Narcissus Called My Name

Narcissus Called My Name

Heroes and the cost of specialness

JOHN J. WHELAN

ISBN: 1548860468
ISBN-13: 9781548860462
Library of Congress Control Number: 2017911188
CreateSpace Independent Publishing Platform
North Charleston, South Carolina

To my friend of thirty years and fellow psychologist, Steve Cann. For all the long conversations about mental health and about the direction of our profession over these many years, I thank you sincerely. The times we have challenged each other's thinking and the many times we have anticipated each other's ideas have truly marked highlights in my professional career.

Contents

Testimonials

Dr. Whelan reveals the hidden consequences of training and service in our military and first-responder organizations, and speaks frankly about why many feel they have "fallen from grace" upon their return to civilian life. Looking beyond PTSD, Whelan brings insights from neuroscience and clinical practice together with veterans' own words to explore how the special status afforded those who serve, and the learned and adaptive ability to suppress emotions when facing chaos or danger, can result in profound alienation from self and others. If the reader wants to truly understand the struggles faced by our military and first responders, they will benefit much from this soundly reasoned book by an experienced clinician and veteran who knows the subject matter inside and out.

Duncan Shields, PhD, University of British Columbia

As a former Basic Training Instructor, all the way through to Leadership Instructor I recognized that John Whelan has hit the nail on the head. The conditioning imposed on those in uniform has a deep and long-lasting effect on those individuals which can easily be exacerbated by an

Operational Stress Injury such as PTSD. Compound this with the forcible removal from the uniformed world into the civilian world and you have a recipe for loss of identity and self-worth as well potential loss of family. Understanding what we do to our own in this narcissistic environment is paramount in understanding how we overcome the potential destructive effects to the individual and their families. This book creates opportunities to begin to understand and to rethink how values need to be adequately reformed, supported, and acted upon.

Steve Crichley, CD, Cofounder Can Praxis

The move away from active duty can be riddled with mental health concerns, addictions, and a soul-crushing loss of purpose, according to Dr. Whelan's interactions, research, and findings. Narcissus Called My Name—Heroes and the Cost of Specialness *will be a difficult read for some; it is frank, eye-opening and a moving documented call-to-action for better proactive, predeployment support, education, services, and discussion—about how we, as a society, treat our veterans, emergency personnel, and first-responders postaction and career. We owe at least that much—to those of us who run toward the emergency.*

Janice Landry, Author:
The Sixty Second Story, The Price We Pay, The Legacy Letters

Narcissus Called My Name *provides powerful insights into the core issues faced by veterans in transition to civilian life: the loss of specialness, identity, and belonging. Dr. Whelan goes beyond popular narratives of combat-related PTSD, demonstrating how the transition out of a military culture deeply impacts those who served.*

Steve Rose, PhD, Eastern Michigan University

Foreword

Canada has a new generation of veterans; men and women who have served in the military, been on multiple postings, and in many cases also deployed to places like Rwanda, Somalia, Bosnia, Haiti, Kosovo, Afghanistan, Libya, or Iraq. We are beginning to recognize some of the impacts from military service and these deployments for veterans and their families. Yet, we continue to grapple with the full consequences of the CAF's increased tempo and scope of deployments since the end of the Cold War and the extraordinary demands placed on individual military members and their families. Many of these effects extend beyond the battlefield and negatively impact veterans' transition to social, economic, and family life back at home.

John is a veteran, a clinician who treats veterans with mental-health problems, and a researcher in his own right. He brings decades of personal, practical, and research experience to the task of disentangling the web that is military mental health and military-to-civilian transition. John and I have had many lively discussions about the issues he covers in his new book *Narcissus Called*

My Name: Heroes and the Cost of Specialness. We have collaborated on research and community events such as a workshop I organized on "Community Stories of War and Peace" and a performance piece I cowrote with female veteran-artist Jessica Lynn Wiebe entitled "The Weight We Share." We see firsthand the pride and professionalism as well as the angst and sense of betrayal that many veterans experience upon their release from the military. We also see the repercussions for family members and their children.

John and I both live and work in a military community. Shortly after I moved to Halifax, Nova Scotia, in 2014, a poster appeared on one of the hydro poles on my street. It read as follows: "*I'm almost thirty. We've been at war with 'terror' since I was in high school. My peers have been to Afghanistan. They've come back paralysed from roadside bombs, mentally scarred from gunning down strangers, and asking: Why are we even over there?*" The poster speaks to some of the negative consequence of Canada's combat participation for youth from Atlantic Canada and included a call to protest the Halifax International Security Forum, an annual meeting of global security leaders. You may disagree with the poster's overt political agenda, but there is no denying that it captures an unease that needs to be addressed. If the poster stirs something in you, read John's book.

What makes Dr. Whelan's book remarkable is his radical commitment to listening, I mean *really* listening, to the stories of those affected, even if they create discomfort. In 2016, Sarah Bulmer and David Jackson—a researcher and veteran–turned-researcher—published an article titled "You Do Not Life in My Skin" in which they stress the importance of listening to stories across difference[i]

Researchers, policymakers, service providers, and the media tend to objectify and pathologize veterans' experiences, which make it hard for veterans to tell their own stories. John empathetically tells the stories of veterans' struggles with mental health, identity, injury, and loss of connection to ask: Is military conditioning itself part of the problem? What if military conditioning—the set of (often gendered) strategies used by militaries to turn civilians into soldiers—sets military members up for failure? If military life hinges on emotional suppression, compartmentalization, and detaching from our inner and outer selves with the promise of specialness and masculine privilege, then what happens to people when these ways of being no longer work, serve a function, and themselves become obstacles to healing and transitioning to civilian life? If so, Whelan suggests we need to offer military members opportunities to unlearn their military identities and "reprogram" themselves. But something larger is required too: moving beyond medical and psychological narratives that tend to medicalize veterans' experiences. What John calls for is not simply a better accounting of the emotional and social costs of military service and a better understanding of their root causes, but a true engagement with Canada's military role in the world. He is critical of a naïve civilian buy-in to the military for the sake of national purpose without linking the geopolitics of Canada's military deployments to their ripple effects across our communities.

As John points out, broader society may be resistant to engage. The stories and analysis he presents bring up disturbing questions about how we condition soldiers, what we expect of them, and how they are rewarded. At the same time, they bring up disturbing questions about how some military members are treated as disposable when they are no longer fit for military deployment. Why does this all matter? Because civilian society is highly invested in our military and we all carry a responsibility to listen and respond. The social contract between veterans, society, and the government has undergone changes over the past decade. Struggles over veterans' policy have been fought at the political front. Not-for-profit organizations have stepped up to fill the gaps in services. Peer-support seems important and effective. But here is what really matters according to John: community and the possibility for (re) connection that it presents. What possibilities are there for genuine connection and for genuine conversation outside of scripted Remembrance Day ceremonies and accolades to veterans?

Rather than just thank veterans for their service, it is time to listen to their stories—even those we find difficult and uncomfortable to hear. John's book is a reminder that sharing stories is as much about listening as it is about telling. As Jessica Lynn Wiebe and I have written in a forthcoming piece, "Sharing the weight of our stories means that someone not only has to hand over the weight by speaking, but that someone also has to take the weight by listening."[ii] John has done exactly this with his therapy groups, but real change requires a broader circle of conversation across military and civilian spheres. The book does not blame or point fingers. It wants to open up space for genuine dialogue and understanding of military service, mental-health problems, and the broader politics of the military in Canadian society. I hope that many of you will be willing to enter this conversation with open minds and hearts.

Maya Eichler
Canada Research Chair in Social Innovation and Community Engagement
Assistant Professor, Political and Canadian Studies/Women's Studies
Mount Saint Vincent University
Halifax

Author's Note

I have spent most of my professional life focused on the military. I served in the Canadian Armed Forces for nearly nine years before leaving to complete undergraduate and graduate degrees and training as a clinical psychologist. In recent years, I have grown increasingly disappointed in how our medical diagnostic system classifies mental distress among soldiers and veterans. Given the decontextualized interventions and cursory clinical training spawned by this system, I believe we must look beyond the *Diagnostic and Statistical Manual of Mental Disorders* (*DSM*) to understand military mental health. I wonder about the effects of military conditioning on our neurobiological wiring, our ability to engage in genuine and intimate relationships, and the effects of this training on our general attitudes and preoccupation with image and self-worth.

My goal is to highlight unanswered questions about the potential effects of military and paramilitary conditioning, especially as they manifest in men and women who have fundamental questions about personal identity. While many experience positive outcomes from military life, a substantial number of veterans experience chronic mental distress. Researchers and clinicians need to consider whether neurological functioning may be affected in some cases more than in others. I believe we should begin to consider specific effects of military conditioning that may alter the ability of some soldiers to recognize and process emotional experiences.

A recent Canadian study reported that about half of our military membership has experienced various forms of childhood abuse and neglect.[iii] Tracey Afifi and her colleagues further speculate that military service may protect these people against self-harm risks unless they experience some form of trauma in the military. Following a trauma, these service members seem prone to a wide range of mental distress, including increased risks of self-harm. And, since we do not pay attention to the neurobiological status of recruits before their service or to the specific effects of military conditioning, we are left with a vaguely defined presumption that deterioration is solely the fault of combat events or due to factors related to their upbringing. These after-the-fact efforts to infer causality risks overlooking what could be the key to understanding negative outcomes for service members. Indeed, the available research seems to point to a pressing need to unravel the complex interplay between developmental histories, military conditioning, trauma exposures, and mental-health trajectories following combat and service.

This book is an accounting of the effects of military conditioning, but it is not a search for someone to blame. After all, I am a product of this conditioning. I joined as a twenty-year-old college dropout, discovered the values of pride and competence, and stayed until just before my twenty-ninth birthday—I became an adult in the military. My awakening to some of the residual aftereffects of my time in the military happened about twenty-five years ago, when my young daughter asked, "Daddy, why are you so angry all the time?" I have had many years since then to try to find the answer for her and for myself—and, more importantly, to stop the behavior. In the end, I think it came down to a black-and-white, rigid, and overinflated sense of myself and my response in instances when I felt trapped and unable to take control through action. Reverting to detachment and aggression as a defensive response was just easier than admitting to vulnerability or helplessness in these situations.

I wrote this book with veterans, first responders, and their families foremost in mind. It is based on the personal stories of actual men and women and meant to capture their words and their experiences to the best of my ability. Given the many theories about mental health and about the problem of PTSD among soldiers and first responders, it was important to challenge common myths by referring to the research literature. Some readers may believe that the discussion of neurobiology at several points is overly academic or aimed at researchers and mental-health clinicians. I believe that it is quite important to outline current debates that challenge some of the information about trauma given to mental-health patients and indeed to the general public.

A Word about the Title

Greek mythology tells the story of Narcissus, a young man who sees his reflection in a river and falls in love with this image, rejecting all others in his preoccupation with himself. He pines away, leaning perpetually over the pool to regard his image, until finally he perishes. In one version of the story, Narcissus ends his own life when he realizes he can never have in physical form the object of his adoration—his own image. I believe that the latter version of the story points to an insidious malady facing many of our younger military veterans—the loss of specialness.

The tale of Narcissus serves as the basis of this book. It speaks to the development of a coveted role—the perfect soldier—fostered by multiple forces within the military that encourage and help move people toward this goal. It also offers a partial explanation for the disorientation and personal loss experienced by many men and women who leave military service. They can develop insatiable ego needs to uphold the persona they have adopted in the interest of meaning and self-worth within their military groups.

Narcissus Called My Name is based on my clinical and research work as a psychologist for serving and retired military over the past twenty-five years. The personal stories of these men and women serve to support the main points of the book. The actual names and some specific details have been altered to protect their anonymity. This book represents my effort to describe the psychological benefits and costs of learning to take on "specialness" as a central aspect of military identity. I believe there can be an unacknowledged downside for many people who are conditioned to become lethal weapons.

Introduction

All members of the Canadian Armed Forces are introduced to a set of specific conditioning rituals designed to transform them into accepted members and representatives of the institution. This training includes exposure to their own capacity for aggression; they need to embrace heightened states of arousal and be awakened to their ability to inflict lethal force on other people when necessary. Soldiers often refer to this conditioning as an on-off switch in instances involving violence. I think about conditioning in aggression as a general attitude of directness, determination and commitment, and an action-oriented focus that may or may not involve violence. In military terms, an aggressive attitude is the propensity to approach challenges and to act/react in measured responses to meet performance demands or perceived threats. This attitude can easily be mislabeled as arrogance. This conditioning is designed to teach soldiers to act automatically under command and to banish vulnerability and basic human reactions from their consciousness.

From the first non-commissioned officer (NCO) barking commands to the first experience of shifting into autopilot to complete a military drill movement, soldiers begin the process of reshaping their neurobiological processes. Military drills, whether on the parade square or on the rifle range, are conducted repeatedly under watchful scrutiny and are designed to move trainees from conscious effort to involuntary reactivity. Even the experience of learning to stand completely still while at attention results in a different experience of the physical body—it must be controlled. Soldiers learn to separate mentally from bodily cues like muscle fatigue, pain, and discomfort and from normal biological processes; they find their private mental places to maintain focused alertness without risking passing out. Recruits also learn the power of the military voice as an instrument designed to project authority. The things that everyday people usually take for granted, like voice tone, inflection, pacing, and volume, are essential elements of this environment. As I heard often during my time in the military, "Even if you have nothing to say, you had better say it loudly and clearly." Finding one's own military voice, a requirement of leadership at any level, is also central to this conditioning. Orders and commands become our security—they signal when to react to threats of any type and when to switch back into prepared alertness, which should not be confused with the experience of relaxation. In my experience, military people and most veterans rarely relax.

This is the point of military conditioning, after all. It is conducted under highly stressful conditions with increasing intensity over time, and it is done repeatedly. The resulting behavioral and accompanying neurological changes continue until our nervous systems develop automatic, hair-trigger reactions to commands and orders. These processes become automated or hardwired to supplant preexisting brain networks—this is the fundamental mechanism behind any learning that produces new behavior.

This conditioning is fostered within environments that also hinge on the lessons of pride and specialness—which we must prove continually—that distinguish us from everyday people and from the people we were upon joining. This attention to pride and specialness at the individual level also reflects the institution's preoccupation with the same things. These beliefs require us to reject who we were before joining to become a better version of ourselves, and they provide the metaphorical bedrock that supports and fosters military conditioning. In all of this, we must also be introduced to our own potential for aggression and the requirements of self-control and restraint under all conditions.

The lessons I have learned over the years, in and out of uniform, have taught me that those personnel who experience adverse childhood experiences (ACE) often become superb soldiers and first responders. I first became aware of this during my clinical internship at the military hospital in Halifax in the early 1990s as part of my master's degree in community/clinical psychology. My training involved several rotations in the psychiatry department and in the addictions rehabilitation clinic located in a separate facility. These departments did not have established professional relationships that presented challenges for my internship. I ended up assessing and treating many of the same soldiers across both departments who were struggling on the heels of their deployments to Somalia and Bosnia, but there were no mechanisms to acknowledge their preservice lives or their military experiences—either they were an addict or they were mentally ill. Many of these men were highly competent and tough soldiers; many of them also came from rough beginnings—abusive, poor, or neglectful families, or faced parental addiction and mental-health problems. This experience had a profound impact on my development as a clinician.

During my doctoral training in the late 1990s, I returned to the military hospital and completed my doctoral dissertation on the mental-health outcomes for soldiers treated for problems with substance misuse. In fact, I served as director for the addictions facility up until 2005, and during this time I established assessment and treatment protocols and training standards for clinicians to begin bridging the gaps between the formal mental health and addictions worlds. In 2005, I left for full-time private practice work to head up a joint initiative sponsored by the Department of National Defence (DND) and Veterans Affairs Canada (VAC) to provide group-based treatment to soldiers and veterans with concurrent addiction and post-traumatic stress disorder (PTSD). This program operated out of our clinic of five psychologists up until 2015 producing several research papers and presentations on our work with veterans.

The things we were discovering from our clinical work with several thousand military veterans were sometimes at odds with the established literature on military mental health. Importantly, the lessons I learned during my first internship about the impact of early development on military mental health continued to be underrecognized when it came to our newest veterans from Afghanistan. I have written two books—*Going Crazy in the Green Machine* (2014) and *Ghost in the Ranks* (2016)—to raise these issues and to highlight the importance of peer and social reconnection among returning soldiers.

I am also of the opinion that soldiers who grew up in challenged environments may be more susceptible to the effects of military conditioning compared to average recruits. In my experience of conducting individual and group therapy with soldiers, those people who struggle with questions over fundamental self-worth are often the ones more likely to invest too much of themselves in the search for special status and to take to extremes the military mental skill set of emotional suppression, compartmentalization, and functional dissociation (detached persona).[iv] I believe it is important to raise the possibility that they may be impaired further via military conditioning—moved further into emotional isolation, calculated rationality, and disconnection from others.

A reality within most first-response and military settings is that there are no stated upper limits on how much one should adapt or sacrifice for the sake of the job. These institutions seem to be always hungry for more commitment from members. Those people without built-in boundaries or the counterbalancing influences of solid family foundations—the ones too willing to prove dependability and self-reliance to impress others—may be at a higher risk of developing mental-health problems. In my view, we will not come to an understanding of military mental health or the transitional strains facing people leaving the military without understanding these basic drives for self-worth and specialness within the cultures of the military and other paramilitary institutions.

Who are these sons and daughters? Many of them grew up in families with military connections who join to become the newest family heroes.[v] Many come from chaotic or abusive backgrounds. Independent of their developmental backgrounds, the majority espouse sincere desires to help other people in need, to protect the innocent, and to uphold and even defend Canadian values. Parents, siblings, and relatives are often incredibly proud of these sons and daughters who decide to serve. Families often share in the investments made by children who have much to prove and have much at stake should they lose this special status—narcissistic wounding.

In *Narcissus Called My Name,* readers are asked to consider the impact of training and mental conditioning on the inner lives of military members and other first responders. The book alerts readers to the mental and emotional costs for those who take on these extraordinary identities and the challenges that often come with the loss of specialness. Some of these stories will be difficult to read; I do believe that they need to be heard if we are to understand the real plight of many of the men and women who have served us.

One

I'm a Military Man

"Hey buddy, I hope you realize that if we start moving you'll be blocking traffic."

Kevin gave an immediate retort: "Why don't you shut your trap and roll up that window before I decide to pull out of that seat!"

There was no response from the other driver. Kevin Skanes continued walking the two hundred yards up to his exit if for no other reason than to show his contempt for the situation. He had decided to drive his daughter to university, and now a blocked highway had trapped him in his truck sweating profusely with a pounding headache. A million thoughts spun in his head over the situation: Where were the goddamned police to clear this up…why were there so many stupid people on the road this morning? Heading up the road had given him something to do about it. There were no comments from the onlookers as he returned to his truck. This time Kevin was on his phone; no help from the police or from the clerk with the traffic division. He started the engine, fully prepared to drive up the center median just as the line of cars began moving. He tramped the gas as he entered the off-ramp to signal to everyone how truly pissed off he was at all of them. Twenty minutes later he was sitting in his driveway, exhausted and still worked up.

Kevin Skanes was a forty-nine-year-old ex-sailor who had retired three years earlier from a twenty-seven-year career and numerous overseas deployments. His time in the military had not been kind to him. The nineteen-year-old physically fit youngster had been replaced by a balding, overweight man with sleep apnea, irritable bowels, and a noticeable limp when he walked. A failed marriage had produced one child, and his on-again off-again common law relationship was a daily reminder about an uncertain future. Kevin had not worked since retiring and had no plans on that front. He spent his days writing to politicians, reading parliamentary reports pertaining to the military, and continually telephoning and e-mailing Veterans Affairs Canada to challenge their policies and services—he was not going to be pushed around anymore.

The former sailor told me about his bitter resentment for never being promoted past the rank of master seaman:

> If things had to be done, I did them. I didn't need anyone telling me what to do, and I wouldn't play the political correctness game when it came to supervising minorities or women. I expected them to do their jobs like the rest of us, or they were useless as far as I was concerned. This got me in a lot of shit with my bosses. The petty officers were always running to the chief boatswain's mate to complain behind my back...if they wanted things done another way they could just go right ahead without me. I made lots of enemies, but let me tell you, I never backed down from a fight. Funny thing was that my name was always on the top of the list when things needed to

be done—RAS [replenishment at sea] deck or jackstay [procedure of transporting people and equipment from ship to ship at sea] supervisor, and boat's Cox'n during all the ship boardings in the Gulf and Swiss Air.

Kevin stops for a moment to calm himself before continuing:

The thing that really pissed me off were the bridge jumpers in Halifax harbour. One morning I heard this jeezly smash as a body hit the water. Sure enough, we had to fish it out and put it on the deck. I saw buddy's face, and I could have sworn it was my cousin from back home... looked identical. I just froze and started swearing and shaking...couldn't stop the shaking. They sent me up to the "fifth floor" [mental-health ward in the Halifax military hospital] because they thought something was wrong with my head. I got diagnosed with depression and PTSD and was handed a bunch of pills. I just threw them in the garbage the same day. Spent nearly three years up there, but they just said I was not going along with the treatment and gave me the boot medically. Only one good thing out of all that...I ended up getting a dog and that's been great...gets me out and helps me forget about being angry. Sometimes I run into those guys I sailed with who want to be friends...they weren't my friend then, and they sure as fuck are not my friend now.

Kevin Skanes grew up in a family the second oldest of seven children. His father came from a long line of east coast fisherman, but he would be the last in a dying industry. He would not be passing his legacy to his sons. His mother ran the house like an RSM (regimental sergeant major). They all had schedules and chore lists and had to get up early even during the summer. As teenagers, the boys were all expected to get jobs to help out. Kevin was a grocery boy at twelve and later joined the cadets with his older brother.

He tells me a little more about his family history: "My mother's father was a Brit [British] who served in the Second World War, but she never said much about that or about him when he got home...she was always wound up...always doing something and had no time for touchy-feely stuff. She taught us to respect our elders, to work hard, and to never be a follower...I still live by those words to this day. Mother was strict, but her and the old man taught us the value of hard work. I'll never forget how proud she was when I signed up."

It was obvious from the outset that Kevin had a well-developed set of personal values, self-reliance, and independence before joining the military. In fact, he was probably too rigid and opinionated even for an organization like the military. Kevin Skanes came from a background that placed primary value on hard work and stoicism—a society of physically able, rough, and ready people. They were uninterested in social niceties, emotionality of any sort, or about the opinions of others. Instead, their value and reputations were based solely on their ability to work and to provide for their families. To Kevin's surprise, however, because of the political nature of military culture, his notions of manhood—the no-nonsense, driven work attitude—were often in conflict with his day-to-day life in the military. Military life can amount to a catch-22 for these members. They are expected to follow orders and complete their duties to the best of their abilities but standing out can garner backlash from others. In an environment where aggressive attitudes must be constrained beneath expectations of subservience and political correctness, these members can face continual frustration and resentment.

Officially, the military expects all members to strive toward excellence. Men and women exist under a dominant, otherwise termed *hegemonic*, masculinity that is reportedly blind to gender and race differences. Language differences are a separate issue since the military seems to play out our national tensions over English-French culture. During my time in the military, many French members endured terrible discrimination and exclusion because of language and Francophone culture. This issue seems to have been resolved, but reluctance to accept differences based on gender and nonwhite status persists in some military units. Even though enrolment rates for English-speaking, white males seems to be on a steady decline, I think we should explore why these things continue to occur despite public pronouncements to the contrary.

Part of the answer lies in the very conception of the Canadian military during the 1870s. In his book, *Manliness and Militarism*,[vi] Mark Moss traced a public relations program designed to overturn perceived lackadaisical attitudes among Upper Canadians and garner support for a standing military with the withdrawal of British forces in 1871. Promoters, empire loyalists, and businessmen fearful of American annexation committed to a massive campaign to stir sentiments of rugged manliness. Their efforts were built upon a fear that real men were being softened by automaton and the conveniences of modern urban life leading to a cultural feminization. Their newly contrived notion of masculinity portrayed Canadian men as rugged outdoorsmen and tamers of the land exerting dominance over the natives, animals, and fauna guided by values reflective of their British breeding. Moss outlines how these notions emphasized patriotism to the crown and chivalrous actions on the battlefield allowing for a direct ideological connection to the storied time of King Arthur. This version of manliness emphasized the importance of war and warriors as invaluable to society—a true man was a soldier. These new militias were made up entirely of males with ideological links to British imperialism and Anglo-Canadian protestant values.

Similarly, the story of the North West Mounted Police, the forerunner to the Royal Canadian Mounted Police (RCMP) also begins as a story of rugged masculinity in 1873. This paramilitary force of mounted riflemen, led by a former military commandant, was tasked to stop the whiskey trade from the United States, to control prairie unrest and the indigenous tribes, and to protect Canadian industry and expansionist interests.[vii]

The creation of this rugged Canadian man was aided ideologically by drawing on a perversion of Charles Darwin's thesis in the mid-1860s. This idea of "survival of the fittest" was advanced by Francis Galton and Herbert Spencer and captured the attention of Victorian England. These ideas about species dominance in the struggle for survival in nature were used to promote notions of militarism and imperialism.[viii] This philosophy emphasized subjugation of weaker races as a practical application of the doctrine. Its offshoot—eugenics—emphasized genetic superiority and provided a necessary rationale for hard, disciplined drilling of Canadian soldiers to enable them to live up to their heritage.

"Men are not militaristic, they become militarized" (Eichler, p. 136). In her book, *Militarizing Men*,[ix] Maya Eichler argued that the promotion of particular masculine values is central to a nation's production of militarized men and women. Indeed, 2017 has been designated as Canada's 150th anniversary, and celebrations are replete with references to our military history meant to unite us once again around these values and to remind us of our place in the world. Eichler's central thesis is also consistent with a theme outlined in this book. Namely, that the conditioning of young men and women in the ideology of rugged masculinity and aggression offers a partial explanation for instances of excessive violence perpetuated by soldiers on others (i.e., sexual assaults, harassment, and bullying) or upon themselves. I would add that these instances are also compounded by an acquired specialness that presupposes a curious mix of subservience and dominance over other people.

Cooper et al[x] argued that there are many forms of masculinities but the military's version centers around hardness, physical and emotional toughness, stoicism, self-reliance, aggressiveness, and a robust sense of heterosexual identity. This form of masculinity is supported by a rigid hierarchy that positions it as the most valuable one. Alternatively, femininity is construed as a gauge against which this masculinity is measured. For instance, displays of weakness, dependence on others, and emotionality are recast as feminine—signs that one is not a real man. In fact, soldiers who cannot suppress emotion after traumatic events are often viewed as compromised men, and by default they are unreliable soldiers. This concern seems to preoccupy the combat arms elements of our military and may offer a partial explanation for the apparent urgency to remove these soldiers from the military.

Interestingly, Matthew Jakupcak and colleagues outlined how behaviors associated with masculine norms are similar to the PTSD symptoms of restricted emotionality and interpersonal detachment during stress.[xi] Traumatized soldiers often show a decreased awareness and differentiation of emotions, difficulties communicating feelings, and a reluctance to seek support from others. In fact, Fox and Pease[xii] argue that these same behaviors are expected of males throughout their lives as signs of manhood; one that is heterosexual, aggressive, authoritative, and courageous. Given these expectations, trauma as a loss of control over oneself is a failure in masculinity, a failure to conform to one's self-concept and assumptions about one's relationship with the world. The soldier who is traumatized must also contend with questions about manhood. Fox and Pease's observations about the *DSM* (*Diagnostic and Statistical Manual of Mental Disorders*) concept of PTSD are nothing short of fascinating. The idea of PTSD was based on Vietnam soldier experiences and focused on individual responses to extreme external events that caused overwhelming emotional distress. The goal was to help remasculinize these soldiers by referring to their reactions as mental wounding—and later as a brain injury—from war and then rehabilitating them to their former status. This approach was decidedly not the case for female PTSD resulting from rapes and other abuses. Leading feminists argued successfully that PTSD among women could only be understood by including the impact of social rules and mores, group and community expectations, and their reactions to female trauma survivors. It would appear then that while PTSD remains solidly couched in scientific language, it is a highly gendered idea about expected reactions to trauma.

This discussion does not discount the profound disorientation and distress experienced by many soldiers and veterans like Kevin Skanes. However, while clinicians trained in the *DSM* paradigm focus on treating damaged brains, or so we think, our veteran clients often have a much bigger goal in mind: salvaging their masculine identity. Soldiers make this abundantly clear through their rejection of various treatment recommendations like expressing emotion, relying on others, or admitting to vulnerability. Many reject the PTSD diagnosis outright because they believe that their postdeployment mental struggles are being reduced to the problems of women or mere civilians.

Sandra Whitworth goes so far as to suggest that military conditioning compels soldiers to "kill off the feminine within themselves" in the service of emotional suppression.[xiii] Whitworth stresses the importance of avoiding an essentialist discussion of masculinity—the presumption that it is a feature of the male gender and conversely that femininity is interchangeable with the female gender. I have seen many cases of women in military and paramilitary organizations (e.g., policing, paramedicine, and firefighting) who uphold masculine values equal to their male counterparts, and there are also many examples of males who uphold feminine value systems. For the most part, however, these men must hide these qualities within their workplaces as a self-protective reaction that becomes quintessentially important when they experience mental-emotional distress.

Kevin's reactions highlight the issue of entitlement as an aspect of his sense of specialness compared to everyone else; asserting control reinforced his ideas about manhood and his military identity. There can be many reasons for impatience and irritation under stress, but as Withworth argued, when military personnel face challenges to their authority and sense of privilege compared to other people, they can resort to threats of physical violence to reestablish control. They often don't see themselves as bound by social rules and norms.

Ciaran Kovach raised an important question when it comes to militaries: How important is sexuality and gender within modern military culture?[xiv] As Kovach outlines, if we believe that aggression, violence, and intense competition for dominance are biologically rooted in males, then soldiering becomes a natural activity for males to channel their natural proclivity for violent and disruptive behavior in defense of their communities. It is a stubborn belief that ignores the reality that many women make wonderful soldiers, military leaders, and first responders. In her study of Canadian soldiers, Lynn Gouliquer argued that women who wish to succeed in the military must also identify with hegemonic masculinity.[xv] They are constantly required to engage in performances of masculinity and femininity, such as revealing or hiding their body parts, dressing conservatively or fashionably, conforming socially, and portraying themselves as sexual and even asexual. Ironically, while women who act more masculine on the job may better fit their work role, they often face negative consequences for doing so. When women transgress socially accepted gender roles, they can face derogatory labels such as frigid, dyke, butch, or mannish.

Gouliquer also reminds us of the public perception that males join the military for glory, duty, and honor, whereas females do it for justice and employment because they are believed to be inherently timid, fragile, and passive. In fact, efforts in Canada to dramatically increase the prevalence of women in our military have already sparked debates that have preoccupied the United States—fears about weakening the fighting spirit through a feminization of military culture. Even so, I believe that the notion of the military as entirely masculine may be an exaggeration. There are numerous examples of military leaders mentoring and caring intensely for the welfare of their subordinates—like their own sons and daughters. I know many senior-ranking people who struggle in retirement because they could not shield or protect their charges from terrible events. Alongside the great demands the military makes of its members, there is a commitment to support and care for its members and their families. While it is true that more can and should be done, Canadian soldiers and veterans benefit from financial supports and medical, housing, and educational services and emotional support initiatives.

Gerard Hofstede is a Dutch psychologist who studied cross-cultural aspects of masculinity and femininity.[xvi] He viewed the former as a national trait emphasizing ambition, acquisition of wealth, and differentiated gender roles. Femininity is seen to be a trait emphasizing caring and nurturing behaviors, sexual equality, environmental awareness, and more fluid gender roles. In high masculine cultures, males are supposed to be assertive, tough, and occupied by material wealth whereas high femininity cultures depict females as modest, tender, and concerned with the quality of life. By this metric, Canada would seem to exist somewhere toward the center of this continuum. There are arenas like business, competitive sport, and the military and first-response organizations where high masculinity values are prized and other places like health care, volunteerism, and community-based organizations where high femininity predominates. However, even within supposed masculine cultures like the military, different units can emphasize varying levels of masculine-feminine ideologies. As noted by others, individual leaders have tremendous effects on the specific ethos/values promoted within their units. These values can also shift dramatically between deployment and in-garrison life. The various uses of masculine or feminine beliefs, then, are arguably determined by the requirements of specific military tasks and roles. The accepted notion of a monolithic military masculinity requires closer examination to avoid overgeneralizations.

When it came right down to it, Kevin Skanes had no language or interest in understanding his emotional life. Exploration of feeling states was irrelevant in his understanding of manhood learned before and during his time in the military. In his mental world, control and dominance over the external environment were paramount. I believe this raises a question about the limits of talk therapies. Namely, I wonder about the extent to which we should focus on emotionality among some military males and females. In Kevin's case, focusing on emotionality would have involved extensive work establishing connections between unexplained somatic symptoms and possible emotional reactions. It would have also meant challenging almost everything he had learned about manhood. Our group work with male soldiers and veterans has taught me that their direct involvement with credible men helps them overcome shame stemming from perceived failures in manhood. They often benefit greatly from reengaging in activities linked with their ideas about masculinity.

The military is a closed society, but it is not ideologically separate from the rest of Canadian society. Our history shows concerted efforts during the early years of the new Dominion to create a needed belief system to lay the ideological groundwork for a military. These beliefs about a Canadian masculinity are promoted widely and are amplified and brought into sharp focus within military and paramilitary institutions. And, they also exist among workers in many traditional industries like oil drilling and construction industries and of course in our national sport. These places may simply provide accessible forums for young men and women to live out our national narrative.

Two

We Are Canada

Another insufferably hot day on foot patrol. It was Dave's turn to take point, leading the six-man section through a crowded market square. Christ, it seemed like every Hodgie was out this morning, he thought. Slow and alert, his comms chirping in his ear in the background—the sounds were irritating and comforting at the same time. "Gun!" Dave had caught sight of a handgun through the maze of people. It was held by a boy probably no more than seven or eight years old. Weapon up. He had already taken the slack out of the trigger, but he hesitated. Dave blinked and looked back knowing he would have to take the shot to protect the guys. This time, no weapon. "Sitrep! Sitrep!" The calls were insistent in his ear. "All clear. Proceed." Dave could not understand what had just happened. Did he endanger everybody by hesitating, or had he just imagined this and nearly killed a child? Chances were that the boy had been set up by someone in the crowd to create a big incident to turn people against the Canadians. It was messing with his head; it was all fucked up. This whole place is fucked up, he thought.

"How could you be that stupid? I can't see how you are my son." Two nights after the market patrol, Dave bolted up from his cot, remembering a long-ago comment from his father. Putting up with his father's anger over minor things had been nothing new for the fifteen-year-old. But that time was different. That time his father had embarrassed him in front of his friends for not closing the cabin door on the family boat. Explanations or excuses of any kind were always ignored, so he simply stopped talking to his father. He hated him and could not wait to get out of there. On his next birthday, despite his old man's comments about the military, Dave was in the cadets. A year after that he was a reserve force infanteer, and his request for transfer to regular force was quickly accepted. He was surprised at how easy military life seemed; it was as if he had been made to be a soldier. He loved the challenges and the adrenaline rush, the weapons, and he excelled in the field. Recognition from his NCOs and respect from younger guys gave him a type of confidence that he had never known. He was a soldier, a man, and he needed nothing from anybody.

But this would all come crashing down here in Afghanistan. After that day, it took everything he had to keep his anger in check. He was losing his mental grip and finally went to see the medical people. He was given one day off, but it only got worse. He was packed up and sent home to Canada. It was over; just like that he was a failure once again.

⌒

Military personnel and first responders of all types take on responsibilities for society that most people either won't or can't. We are required to prove ourselves worthy of these special roles—to be the ones who run toward danger and chaos when others run away, and we commit to put our lives on the line for our brothers and sisters in uniform and for strangers alike. During our time in uniform, we are repeatedly reminded that we are special, despite the day-to-day realities that can sap our souls. We deal with inconsistent, conflicting, and even arbitrary rules, great leaders or self-interested ones, and we continually cycle between full-on panic situations and bone-crushing boredom. We really have to find ways to ignore all this other stuff to keep putting our best efforts forward and avoid being worn down. Many strive to be the star performers—at or near the top of training courses, receiving early promotions, being the go-to person, and being respected by subordinates and superiors.

Within systems where the goal is perfection, people can turn into rigid, overcontrolled obsessive types. Well, in retrospect I certainly became one in my NCO roles. Our outward displays of competence, toughness, or even cockiness often masks a constant anxiety about having to keep it all from crashing in on us. We can be suddenly thrown into new roles where we immediately must show that we know what we are doing to have the confidence of our superiors and subordinates alike. In effect, we masquerade hoping that nobody notices until we figure out what we are doing. I think an odd thing happens here. Even if we do not believe that "we are all that," we have little choice but to pretend that we are confident and competent. Often, it is only when the real thing happens and we manage effectively that we develop confidence. This is especially true for those selected for special training or duties. So, an exterior that hides these fears of being exposed as incompetent leads people to overstate their confidence and assuredness, which can certainly appear as narcissistic self-interest. As one Afghanistan veteran quipped sarcastically in an interview recently, "What is the reward for doing an outstanding job? More and more until you crack or reach your level of incompetence. The system is always hungry for more."

Every leader has his or her favorite go-to soldier, and nobody wants to let them down. This is a powerful motivator, especially given the risks of being embarrassed in front of peers. We should not forget that despite the talk about brotherhood, there are always people who secretly want to see us fail. Envy or personal dislike means that other people will take covert steps to undermine the chosen one—blading. This is just the way it is in a highly competitive system.

Our lives are governed by a perpetual state of prepared alertness even when it is not required in our daily activities. The patch on our shoulders means that we are the ambassadors representing Canada on the world stage. We are trained and reminded constantly that we are members of special societies set apart from the broader society—we are the guardians, the protectors, and the sheepdogs. We are convinced that we are a cut above our civilian counterparts—that they are lazy, undisciplined, and self-interested compared to us. They cannot be trusted to understand us or to offer us anything that we do not already possess. Such assumptions predominate in the inner worlds of military and first responders of all stripes, because the development of big personalities and big ego needs is normal in their professional environments. But the accepted notion that civilians are not ethical, hardworking, or moral people is unfair and simply not true. There are numerous examples of good men and women all around. They just don't pound their chests about it. They live their lives anonymously and quietly, supporting their families and communities throughout the country.

Members of the military and other first responders don't appreciate the fact that higher ideals are meant to unite us in a common purpose and to control us, especially when it comes to the use of force. An unfortunate outcome is that military members can truly believe that they are the holders and protectors of society's moral conscience, while the very people who are served come to be viewed suspiciously. Maybe this is part of the reason why military people and veterans appear disconnected from society and even detached and arrogant in their interactions. We had to earn pride in ourselves and in the institution's ideals to protect ourselves from the threat of shame that can come from not measuring up. A typical military insult is illustrative here: "You are just a flat-faced civvie wearing the uniform."

As the Afghanistan War fades into yet another shadowy memory, we appear to have two parallel and competing narratives to explain mental distress among those who served there—the injured warrior brain narrative and the childhood trauma narrative. The literature is replete with examples of flip-flopping between these explanations. We are not yet at a point of understanding how to integrate these competing narratives into a coherent accounting of postwar or postservice declines. We seem to be at an impasse. Politically, the national cliché of the self-sacrificing, stoic Canadian soldier means that we do not want to blame soldiers—our professed heroes—for having done their jobs. On the other hand, many soldiers with lingering distress and mental-health problems consistently relay stories about events that cannot be reduced to combat. Conversely, many of their stories point to intimate and complex relationships between their military experiences and their early lives, which are usually never examined outside of private therapy offices.

Here's my point: The mental building blocks for an operational mental injury may be set in motion long before critical events ever happen. These ingredients can be rooted in early development and amplified through military conditioning, but they are also present among those soldiers who come from stable, nurturing families. Essentially, most soldiers develop adaptations (i.e., emotional suppression, compartmentalization, and a detached persona) to help them succeed in training and to do their jobs. Unfortunately, these same adaptations that served them wonderfully in carrying out their military duties can interfere with the normal processing of both routine and unusual events. Furthermore, the same embodied adaptations and the overinvestment in military specialness seems to underpin the problem of maladjustment to civilian life. We need to move beyond our clichés if we are to understand post-service maladjustment.

This specialness or narcissistic preoccupation, often construed pejoratively, can be viewed as an adaptation to manage self-worth needs. In institutions like the military, RCMP, and other first-response organizations, we do not talk about these aspects of personality, since they are valuable and expected. Those people who are self-assured, decisive, confident, and able to switch off and ignore the emotional needs of others and themselves are in high demand within these systems. The fact that a high percentage of star performers very often experienced varying levels of childhood abuse and neglect should come as no surprise. They are often the tough and resilient ones. Even those who border on being renegades within their units are highly valued because of their innate abilities to perform under extreme pressure.

Within the military, while leaders and peers value rough and irreverent personalities, they are rarely acknowledged formally by the system through promotions, awards, or special attention. These soldiers represent a stark contradiction to the stereotype of the quietly confident and unassuming, professional soldier. We cannot seem to accept this contradiction publicly without appearing to undermine the image of our military institution or, on the other hand, without risking being misunderstood as blaming these soldiers for postdeployment or postservice problems. We should address these misconceptions head-on and engage in a meaningful dialogue about the public-private worlds of soldiers and veterans.

Service members who experienced childhood adversity sometimes carry significant shame, disavowed outrage, and damaged self-worth that they work to overcome and to actively forget. They want to have a new beginning without the baggage from their past lives. Childhood adversity is not restricted to military enrollees either. For example, published estimates place developmental abuse rates at 38 percent of paramedics,[xvii] 30 percent of mental-health clinicians, 20 percent of police officers,[xviii] and 34 percent of family physicians.[xix] For many of them, the promise of specialness and recognition from those in authority can be intoxicating for their reinforcing effects. All of us, at one time or another, have experienced the glow of social approval and its power to offer us a glimpse of a new way of being in the world. These experiences are relevant and needed, and many veterans report going to extraordinary lengths to avoid losing access to this specialness.

I have seen repeatedly in my clinical work and research with ACE/OSI (adverse childhood experiences/operational-stress injuries) military and first-responder clients that it is quite common that long-forgotten and unwanted memories are often activated during and after critical military events.[xx,xxi] Whether these reactions represent a new narcissistic injury—the insight that they are essentially weak and alone—or serve as reminders of things they have been attempting to forget is a matter of debate and a relevant topic for ongoing research. The point is that when they are activated emotionally, they automatically attempt to revert to their military conditioning to maintain control. They work to contain very common reactions like anger, compassion, despair, and the peculiar reaction of betrayal that seems to be pointed at the failures of specialness to protect them.

These *ACE people*, for lack of a better term, are often the ones more likely to double down on their military skills of emotional suppression and compartmentalization, often turning into the workaholics in efforts to protect their military personas. They invest considerable effort in this regard—never refusing a job or a posting—often at the cost of family relationships and their physical and mental health. They tend to see the military experience as the only real family they have ever known, which probably explains their comments about feeling abandoned and forgotten when it ends.

To be clear, the ability to suppress one's immediate emotional reactions can be highly adaptive in managing chaotic situations and for personal survival. When these strategies are overused, however, there is often a trade-off in the form of weakened introceptive skills—the ability to recognize one's internal states.[xxii] Our clinical work with veterans shows that they seem to be at increased risk of developing unexplained somatic issues like gastrointestinal problems, persistent muscle tension, chronic headaches, reduced libido, and, of course, obsessional thinking. Among the many veterans with these concerns, they are often highly rational, intellectual, and externally focused. They usually do not engage in personal self-reflection, which translates into an inability to name their internal experiences and emotional states—alexithymia.

As a species dependent on symbols and language, we name things in our environment to have dominion over them. This process of naming also applies to our internal world. In fact, the inability to recognize or to name our internal reactions—to pay attention to our mental life—can contribute to a sense of loss of control and even confusion about our basic identity. In my experience, people who habitually suppress their internal reactions risk wearing out mentally and emotionally. Some are often plagued by thoughts of suicide that are driven by impulses unknown to them. In their private worlds, they cannot envision any other alternatives.

The upside of learned specialness is that it can also serve as a type of protective barrier from self-worth damage from earlier abuses and neglect. For some people, military experiences can override or even resolve fundamental questions of worth and basic value—they come to a new understanding of themselves in the world. For many others, however, a fall from grace—the loss of their military reputations—presents them with the same questions about self-worth that they hoped to overcome by joining in the first place. Many veterans believed that they were social misfits. They were bullied, had difficulties with authority, were uninterested in school, or they had a different value system compared to their peers. If they are released from service because of mental problems, the experience can compound these fears over lack of belonging and even fundamental worthlessness. Despite years of involvement with talk therapies and medications, many of these people remain emotionally isolated and lonely. Disconnection from their inner worlds means that they are also disconnected from other people.

I have long wondered whether this preoccupation with specialness, while serving as the basis for pseudoconnection to others, represents a basic need to overcome fears of worthlessness. John Cacioppo, a psychologist who has studied loneliness, made this exact point in a recent article: "Loneliness, interestingly, is related to an increase in egocentrism. Self-preservation depends more on your attention to your outcomes when you're lonely than when you have lots of connections."[xxiii] I believe his observations can apply generally and among military personnel despite the gregarious nature of the organization. Cacioppo argued that the solution does not simply come down to placing people together or even teaching them social skills. Alternatively, there need to be opportunities for genuine interconnectedness. This is incredibly difficult in military and first-response settings where vulnerability must be hidden and denied. This suggests to me that the repair of narcissistic injury, which I believe lies at the root of ongoing trauma reactions, can only be accomplished by changing the nature of relatedness within these primary groups.

Above all else, female and male soldiers learn the values of traditional masculinity, including self-reliance, stoicism, and a belief in ourselves to get things done. When it comes to militaries, the value system reinforces the centrality of rigid beliefs and ethos, black-and-white thinking, uncompromising discipline, and prepared alertness. Soldiers are taught how to moderate normal stress reactions along the so-called flight-fight continuum by learning how to harness adrenaline surges and to transform them into automatic, aggressive action under command. Essentially, soldiers actively participate in changing their brain's wiring for the promise of specialness—being among the chosen. Again, it is important to emphasize the point that this conditioning is required to produce capable soldiers.

Three

You Don't Get to Bash the Military

"Before you go too far here, I want to make a couple of things clear. I've seen lots of shrinks over the years inside and outside the military...had lots of time to think. Ya know when it comes right down to it, two things have kept me alive till now—drinking and joining the army when I was twenty." This was Mary's second session with Jerome, an Afghanistan veteran, and she was working very hard to show him that she was on his side. Her efforts included several comments reflecting her anger and dismay about how the military had treated him. She was surprised at Jerome's defense of the military.

Jerome continued:

When I think back, I grew up learning that I could not trust my old man because of his drinking. So, I learned early on to fight my own battles. Being good in school was the only bright spot even though the schoolyard was like a war zone for me. By the time I was in my teens, a couple of things happened that kinda changed things...I saw a school friend and his brother killed in a motorcycle accident, and a year later my closest friend ended up killing our neighbor when he was drunk out of his mind...So I'm about sixteen, and one night I was drinking and this urge comes over me to just go kill myself, right out of the blue. Scared the shit out of me. Got to sleep that night, but when I woke, it was still there, and it stayed every day after that and got worse and worse... The only way to quiet it down was to drink and smoke a bit of weed so that is what I did just to keep going. Did that for a couple of years, and when the chance to join the military came along, I thought what the hell. I had nothing to lose. Thinking back on it now, it was the best decision I ever made. They taught me how to be proud of myself, forget about that other stuff, and just focus on what was in front of me...I loved it, loved the adrenaline, loved deployments, and just being with guys who were just as crazy as me. I could absolutely count on them. What did me in was being promised a promotion and a low tempo posting and then at the last minute being told to gear up again for another deployment or say good-bye to my career...That did me in, I think. Old thoughts of just ending it all came back, and suddenly the place that I called home was alien to me. There was no place to put my anger, so back to the booze and here I am.

Jerome's story is not very unusual at all. It does not mean that everyone who joins the military or who takes on other first-response roles have challenged upbringings. But, at the same time, such a background can serve these individuals very well in managing demanding roles. During my time in uniform, we had the benefit of supervisors who mentored us and reminded us that military life was also a game to be played. In effect, we were expected to do our jobs well—to jump when ordered—but not take it too seriously or personally. In one way, then, military life is a type of public performance, and the object of the performance is to display subservience while keeping our true opinions or misgivings to ourselves. But I also think that when we begin to take the game seriously, out of necessity, we can get lost in these roles. In some respects, this experience is similar to that of movie actors who speak about becoming disoriented through the roles they take on and the mental distress they can experience as they attempt to shed the aftermath of dark characters. For example, in the movie *Apocalypse Now*, which depicted the psychological quagmire of the Vietnam War, the actor Martin Sheen reportedly experienced a heart attack attributed to the mental-emotional distress linked with his role. Similarly, even though soldiers may understand that they are playing roles, they can internalize them to such an extent that their psychological stability can be derailed.

I believe that this situation is a significant challenge for soldiers and first responders to navigate and it presents a real social dilemma. While it is a noble and necessary calling to take on roles for the betterment and safety of general society that hinge on taking action in the face of danger, there are few places for these people to decompress from these roles. To say that these organizations represent the last bastions of traditional masculinity would be an unhelpful cliché. Of course, there are times and places where tough, immediate, and decisive actions are necessary regardless of the sensibilities of other people. This is not at issue. The shortcoming of this notion of real manhood, however, in Anglo societies at least, is the expectation to ignore one's reactions and simply move on. These expectations can serve as a fundamental setup for the well-publicized notion of self-stigma.

Instead of being portrayed as an individual shortcoming, self-stigma can best be considered as internalized social stigma—judging oneself by the reactions and attitudes about mental health held within one's primary groups.[xxiv] Indeed, those military members who may need reassurances or opportunities to decompress with others are often viewed as being less than the expected ideal. These days, they risk being immediately identified as having a mental-health problem. In understaffed and pragmatic working environments where legitimate and very human reactions cannot be acknowledged, these people must be aberrant. I would argue that this setup for reactions of shame serves as the basis for self-stigma.

The motivations to take on social protector roles can be rooted in many things in a person's preservice life. For instance, in one UK study of paramedic trainees, 94 percent of them had been exposed to injury and accidental deaths prior to entering training and a substantial number already met the criteria for PTSD.[xxv] While these experiences may have prompted their decision to enter first-response roles, the point I wish to make here is that the actual training is done with our primary group's forefront in our minds—military, police, paramedics, or firefighters. These groups focus on teaching members to internalize codes of conduct and values that apply to everyone—it must be this way to ensure expected performance standards and to foster group specialness. We should not forget either that in military groups, at least, public sanctioning for mistakes or substandard performance is a valuable training tool. This means that individuals must learn to submit to group norms—often described in the academic literature as conforming to the "tyranny of the group." People can lose track of themselves and be swept along with the goals, values, and needs of the group. This also has direct implications when it comes to lawful commands.

The distinction between lawful and illegal "superior orders" was at the root of the Nuremberg trials following the end of World War II. In the end, neither senior commanders nor average soldiers could escape punishment by using the defense of following orders to explain their roles in committing atrocities. This distinction is the focus of research in the United States aimed at understanding moral injuries among soldiers.[xxvi] In our modern-day military, however, soldiers tell me that it is incredibly difficult and risky to question orders or to refuse to comply with commands. Those who do make these choices—even if their refusals to comply are warranted or if they take morally correct but unsanctioned actions—can find themselves quickly on the outside of the military. So, in the interests of allegiance to the group, soldiers must also be willing to betray their own values if needed—to turn a blind eye to events to protect the entire group or agree to engage in questionable activities by turning off their own moral compass. They are welded to their groups as the holders of legitimacy.

Veterans describe many instances of moral dilemmas and mental injuries from their time in various places, including Somalia, Rwanda, Bosnia, and Afghanistan. They tell me that notions of right and wrong can become relative or meaningless terms. Many of them are tortured not by specific events but instead by the mental strategies they had to use to survive. A veteran who was active in Rwanda told me, "In my mind, I had to turn all these people, including women and children, into animals to keep from going crazy…We should have done something to help."

For many people, the power and control of the group occurs largely out of their conscious awareness; those who do see it and attempt to resist by retaining their individuality are almost universally singled out as potential problems. The stability and ego interests of the group mean that outliers cannot be tolerated because, as weak links, they have the potential to undermine the integrity of the group. People learn to project personas that are evaluated and either accepted or rejected by the group and its leaders. Some people believe mistakenly that higher rank will enable them to overcome this control and allow them to stand against the group if necessary to do the right things—to follow their private moral compasses. An army veteran said to me, "I thought that when I became a warrant, I would be able to protect the young ones, but I was even more powerless in that role." Some people did take these risks and paid the price in terms of denied promotions, postings, and worse. Many simply became aware that, as they seemingly gained more power, the pressures to conform often shifted away from in-your-face challenges to other control tactics like rumors and covert assaults on their established reputations. This means that soldiers regardless of rank learn to present themselves as compliant yet confident and self-reliant people in order to protect themselves within their respective groups. It also means that they must invest a strong personal belief in this public persona to carry it off convincingly or risk being identified as a faker, a nonbeliever: "*Smarten up. Do you think this is some sort of game?*"

Interestingly, no matter how they leave the military, most veterans are often the strongest defenders of the military system of training. In part, I believe this is done to protect our own investments and legacies; none of us wants to entertain the idea that we may have wasted our time. It also allows us to remain mentally connected to our former units and buddies. In this way, even as veterans we do not have to face the prospect of being truly alone. The thought of questioning the relevance of military values can seem insurmountable because it means having to acknowledge the personal prices we paid for life in uniform. Relinquishing these engrained values also comes with the risk of being completely adrift in civil society.

I believe that the learned skill of compartmentalization fosters this private-public splitting to some degree. Ironically, within their groups, soldiers are almost expected to criticize orders and their leaders—a pissed-off sailor is a happy sailor—but they will defend the military instinctively to outsiders. In effect, being angry or even irreverent can be expected signs of commitment to the institution. It is a peculiar notion of loyalty in a black-and-white system where complexities, paradoxes, and even some legitimate grievances cannot be acknowledged. Many soldiers and veterans end up flip-flopping between anger and disappointment on the one hand and allegiance to military values on the other. One veteran told me, "The system is really screwed up, but we did a great job regardless and I am proud of that." Readers might be surprised that many soldiers believe that they often have to covertly work against complex official policies for the welfare of their groups and to protect the integrity of the system. At other times, these soldiers can be given unofficial permission to bend rules to get things done. In such cases, they might hear a command like, "I don't care how you do it. Beg, borrow, steal, but I want it done...and I don't want to know the details."

Four

Bring Us Some Heroes

We like to be reminded that our central calling,
our main task on this planet, is the heroic.

—Ernest Becker[XXVII]

The faint dub-dub-dub of helicopter rotors grew louder as it scooted across the darkened landscape; it was a risky nighttime insertion. Captain Roger Beland and his infantry corporal were to be dropped well beyond their assigned coordinates, leaving them a two-day hump to get on station. As Beland and his partner began their march, he wondered what he was doing here. Most of his fifteen years in uniform had been on field exercises in Canada, but in the build-up to the First Gulf War he had volunteered for training in Kingston with the intel section before this deployment. And here he was traipsing around the desert as a newly minted intelligence officer. His orders were clear—act as the eyes and ears on the ground in the border region between Iraq and Kuwait.

Early morning on day three, the familiar sound of small-arms fire in the distance signaled that their trek was at an end. As they scurried between burned vehicles and damaged buildings, Beland turned a tight corner to be faced with a young male, maybe fifteen or sixteen years old, turning to aim his weapon at him. Beland's reaction to the shock was immediate; his sidearm snapped to shoulder level. Crack! Crack! Two rounds were instantly off in the kid's direction—one bullet entered the upper chest, the second into his left cheek. Down he went. Without looking at his partner, Beland simply announced, "Keep moving!"

Captain Beland had made this comment to his stunned young compatriot nearly two decades earlier. He tells me that at the time, he had felt nothing. In fact, if anything it had felt right to do the job; after all, it was a war, he was a soldier, and this kid was an armed combatant. I asked him why this was bothering him after so many years. He responded, "At the time, I really was gung ho. People told me that I was too hard to get along with, too opinionated, and even too self-absorbed. I had to be those things…But nobody could ever say that I did not look out for my guys." Roger tells me that he is not that guy anymore, that as the father of two teenage boys he could not imagine losing either of them: "So now a little brown kid from halfway around the world that I saw for maybe ten seconds comes back to haunt me almost every night." I ask him, metaphorically, what this kid from his dreams wants from him. Roger is quick to answer me: "He wants me to pay the price for killing him, and I don't know how to pay for that. Maybe he wants my life to square the debt. I don't know…You know, the only person who knew about this was the corporal who was with me. Jeez, I can't even remember his name…Anyway, I heard he was killed in Afghanistan a bunch of years ago, so I am the only one left with this."

In his acclaimed book *Denial of Death*, Becker[xxviii] asserted that human nature prepares each of us to fill the world all alone if needed, even if our minds shrink at the thought. Each of us are destined to repeat the tragedy of Narcissus because we are hopelessly preoccupied with ourselves. This human quality—narcissism—is what keeps men marching into gunfire in wars. Secretly, every soldier must believe that he is the special one who will be spared and not die. He only feels sorry for the man next to him. Even altruistic selflessness can be an extension of the desire to be the revered hero—to live on in the minds of others because of his deeds.

How do we fit Becker's opinion of the human condition with the sentiment of many soldiers who've told me that they did not fear dying? Instead, they often describe willingly accepting the possibility of death for the greater good of their comrades and for mission success. One hypothesis is that even though their physical bodies might be sacrificed, they believed they would live on in the minds of others because of their heroic deeds on the battlefield. After all, this is a central part of the Canadian hero narrative. As a retired army veteran told me, "I wanted to get to Afghanistan to show them all that I was a good soldier…to be with the guys. If I had gone, there was no way I was coming back alive."

Words like *honorable death, ultimate sacrifice, uncommon valor,* and *bravery* are near-mystical ideals in Canada that may serve to override the gut-wrenching human fear of one's physical obliteration. Heroism and altruistic self-sacrifice can become the means by which any soldier—or any of us for that matter—can vanquish fears of irrelevance and even our own physical deaths. Even so, I still think we are left with questions about the source of the fear that is believed to be at the root of military PTSD. Maybe these soldiers learn to banish their true fears of dying and are simply denying the presence of danger. I think it is quite possible that their conditioning in aggression, essential to all militaries, means that fear becomes unrecognizable; fear is experienced as a series of physiological reactions that are harnessed and used as energy to keep moving forward regardless of the circumstances.

In his book, *Once a Warrior, Always a Warrior,* Charles Hoge[xxix] provides a detailed description of the psychological conditioning of American soldiers in Vietnam. He argues that the greater fear experienced by veterans—often confused with PTSD—was that their deeds and hence their lives would end up in futility. On a somewhat related clinical thread, the psychiatric literature has described PTSD as a narcissistic injury—any event that exposes one's hidden, true self, especially when there is an experience of a "fall from grace" and the loss of specialness.[xxx] It has also been suggested by psychodynamically trained clinicians that these narcissistic injuries often result in the experience of rage. At a surface level, this internal struggle is often seen among people who always seem to be angry toward others or over external events. At a deeper level, this wrath and hatred is directed at the self.

How does this notion of narcissism relate to mental decline among soldiers and veterans? I believe that mental distress comes down to specific events where the things done or not done by them shake their fundamental beliefs in specialness and personal heroism. Members who believe that they failed often direct anger at others or take it out on themselves in various ways. For example, I saw a sailor years ago who was referred by a civilian doctor because of unexplained and repeated injuries to his right hand. His career was winding down after a lifetime of deployments, and he had no plans for civilian life. I asked him the usual questions about his upbringing and his military service. He told me about growing up in a home with a physically violent father and that he left to join the military as soon as he was old enough. He was extremely proud of the fact that he was not like his father because he never raised his voice in anger to another person even while in the military. I asked him how he managed the usual tensions of sailing and his relationships with his wife and children. He responded, "In the navy, I would just ignore insults and stupid people and focus on my job, even stupid jobs like the Swiss Air thing…Now that I'm out, at home I just go to my workshop and wait for things to blow over." When I asked him what he did when he was really upset, he stared at the floor: "I take my hammer and hit my hand as hard as I can to get my mental stability back." For a man who could not acknowledge the experience of anger even when it was warranted without being reminded of his father, then, his only acceptable outlet was self-directed harm. Despite my efforts to provide him an explanation for his way of managing anger—maybe even to protect other people—he never returned. I think it was simply too shameful an admission for him to face me afterward.

Many of the struggles veterans face involve a constant cycling between reactions of anger and despair that can come with a loss of perceived specialness. Their anxieties and even panic reactions seem reminiscent of Becker's main argument: fear of the ultimate purposelessness of one's life. We will all die, and our lives and deeds will be forgotten with the passage of time. The struggle for veterans—and for all of us for that matter—seems to come down to overcoming fears of lack of relevance and finding the enthusiasm and humility to enable us to participate fully in life with other finite beings. As a social species, then, the only reprieve from ultimate despair seems to be genuine interconnectedness with other people.

Five

After the Glory

The blistering heat of the desert sun threatened to sap Derrick's mental focus at the checkpoint. At nineteen years old, he had almost two years under his belt as a soldier before deploying to Afghanistan. Derrick had to stay alert because the locals were always pushing the limits—either they did not understand the rules, or they resented these foreigners and couldn't care less, or else they just wanted to test the Canadians. But you could never be sure; any of them could be a bad guy. He had already intercepted several cars and motor-bikes earlier in the morning and turned them around without inci-dent. Maybe it would stay quiet till the end of his watch, he thought. The brief mental break was interrupted by the sight of dust kicking up behind a little red car approaching from the distance. The car came closer, up to the cement barrier and the sign with written in-structions to stop. Derrick gave a second warning by hand signal, but the car continued barreling toward him. Three rounds erupted from his C7 (Canadian assault rifle), two of them hitting the driver in the upper torso, killing him. The third ricocheted off the car, heading off somewhere to the right of the car.

The errant round would continue for another seventy-five yards before finding an unintended target in the form of a young girl playing in the dirt. It ripped a gash across her left cheek before thudding into the ground beside her. Amid the chaos of soldiers setting up a perimeter and others running toward the vehicle, Derrick had not noticed the sound of screaming until he saw the woman holding her injured daughter. He was confused by the sight of the bleeding youngster; his chest squeezed tightly, but he was quickly distracted by his sergeant's hand on his shoulder: "Great job." Derrick got the same reactions from his buddies and his commanders for following protocols exactly. It was better to say nothing about his fleeting reaction and just go along with being the designated hero of the moment. It was easier to just slip back into the section: "Ramped up, amped up, rock an' fuckin' roll." Of course, he had done the right thing; this was what he had trained for. This was the real deal as a Canadian soldier, and he had pulled it off textbook. File that other shit away, and carry on with the rest of the guys, he thought.

Within the section, this was all the other guys wanted to talk about, especially when the engineers found a stash of weapons and explosives in the backseat and trunk of the car. There was talk about Derrick being given a commendation and possibly being nominated for a medal for his quick action. Derrick wasn't sure why he did not want to talk or to even think about it anymore. Truth was he barely remembered pulling the trigger because of the fear of fucking up. It all just seemed to happen automatically, just another Figure 11 (cutout silhouettes of an attacking soldier used for training purposes). It happened to have been the right thing to do, but it could just as easily have been the wrong thing if one of his rounds had set off the explosives in the car. He didn't want to think about that too much.

It can be a terrible dilemma to do the right thing and have it simultaneously end in unintended yet terrible outcomes. It is the stuff of torment and nightmares. How do soldiers find a way out of these traps? The safest position is to reset and move back into a mental focus on rules of engagement (ROEs), tactics and strategy, maintaining focused situational awareness, and staying on top of the adrenaline. Remaining hyperfocused on required tasks is essential since second-guessing has no place in a war zone. When it does become safe to come out of adrenaline mode—which many dislike intensely— soldiers can be left in an unwelcome world of replaying events and second-guessing. The things that made absolute sense when they were locked in and charged up often take on entirely different meanings.

I recently had a long conversation over coffee with my friend, retired Royal Canadian Air Force Captain Medric Cousineau. Medric is a recipient of the Star of Courage for his heroic actions during a 1986 nighttime rescue at sea, which he outlined in his book *Further Than Yesterday*.[xxxi] He gave me permission to quote his observation that "medals cast a long shadow" to explain the unrealistic expectations projected onto identified heroes, who may also be thinking, all I was doing was trying to stay alive. Medric told me about knowing many other military medal recipients who had lingering mental-health struggles, including PTSD. It is easy to presume that the events that led to the awarding of medals in the first place led to these issues. He explained that being singled out like this puts many of them in a terrible bind. The notoriety that comes with this level of attention—being anointed publicly—comes with an unspoken expectation that you could do this again and again because now you are superman. You automatically become the example of excellence. There is no room to admit to fears, vulnerabilities, or even self-doubts about what happened. If these men and women decide to reach out to formal mental health–care providers to make sense of things, they enter a foreign world.

Open dialogue, civility, and implied trust—these well-meaning expectations are introduced to people who seek help for mental distress related to their military service. But these notions and the acknowledgment of possible moral or spiritual injury are diametrically opposed to warrior mentality. I have been told by many soldiers, in fact, that the downside of talk therapy is that they lose their sense of anger. This loss is viewed negatively, because anger was their friend, protector, and primary motivator in nearly all aspects of their lives. Anger and a no-holds-barred aggressive attitude are an important part of specialness. But if they do not want to reflect beyond the initial experience of adrenaline, situational awareness, and making a decision about whether to take some action or to risk being emasculated as a weakling, they can face a forlorn existence. Other things like treating one's fellow man or oneself with compassion and forgiveness or seeking personal redemption for unforgiveable deeds can cease to be part of the conversation, leaving them to carry these things. When left unvoiced, reactions of guilt and self-doubt can erode their self-confidence and contribute to social withdrawal and a range of mental-health struggles.

When it comes to soldier distress, biological explanations help us to avoid these awkward conversations about possible institutional setups for existential crises. A Bosnian veteran told me, "The medical people explained that all my anger came from the stress of the deployment...that I had a kind of brain injury but I don't know. We were supposed to be there to intervene under the blue [United Nations], but all we did was sit back and listen to the screams and never-ending gunfire...men, women, and children...We were just as guilty as those drunken bastards running around slaughtering people." We typically respond to these very human dilemmas facing soldiers by looking for distorted beliefs about responsibility, how they might have felt powerless, helpless, or terrified, and whether these reactions might signal a diagnosis of PTSD because of presumed damage to their brain circuitry. We instruct them to retell cryptic versions of their stories until they are desensitized to things like devastation or despair over the deaths of women and children—reducing these tragedies to mere bad memories. I suppose this is better than leaving them to a life of torment. We must do more than simply convince them that there is something they are doing or not doing now that is causing lingering distress. I believe that we need to encourage their complete unedited stories and take seriously the importance of their military conditioning in understanding their struggles.

As professional helpers, we are all taught the essential skill of concerned detachment—to approach our clientele tentatively and to not overinvest or overidentify with them. This means that we usually don't consider the legacy of war and other deployment experiences on soldiers as people. After all, most helpers have never experienced anything similar. To convince soldiers and others to become desensitized to the suffering of others, in my mind, makes everyone just a bit less human. I suppose in a secular world we cannot offer much more—well, maybe our own compassion and courage to share the loads of what they have experienced on our behalf. And this comes with its own risks for caregivers—compassion fatigue.[xxxii]

Last year, I served as coleader of a research project into veteran mental health. My academic colleagues and I also wanted to hear from seasoned trauma clinicians. We were surprised by their descriptions of things like unexplained anxieties, sleep disruptions, and unexplained bouts of crying related to their work. Like their veteran clients, they also described fears of asking for help because of mistrust and strong reactions of helplessness and frustration. In a paradoxical twist, then, trauma clinicians can find themselves ending up in the same place mentally as their military clients. They can end up paralleling their emotional and psychological worlds—powerless and isolated. All their "self-care" activities could not protect them from these reactions. I believe this is partly because soldiers present unsolvable problems as defined by a medicalized understanding of mental distress, which does not account for the effects of military conditioning.

Many helpers, family, and friends don't risk engaging these people on a human level. They don't risk sharing the messiness of their torments or trying to understand how these events probably challenged everything their patient or loved one believed about humankind and instances of good in the world. After all, such an approach might also challenge their own cherished beliefs. In a world of sterile, evidence-based treatments—and we do need evidence about what works—attention to this kind of messy and upsetting stuff has not been supported. Instead, practitioners have risked turning soldiers and other "heroes" into victims of their biology and consumers of interventions; in the process, they have inadvertently enabled ongoing self-absorption. Given the limitations of our present solutions—most Canadian soldiers treated for operational-stress injuries never return to their workplaces, and they often continue to suffer as veterans—medical practitioners seem to be in desperate need of innovative alternatives.

Instead of fostering victimhood among veterans, health-care providers can engage with them directly and candidly, providing them meaningful responsibilities within their groups and their families. Concerns about relevance and lost specialness need to be addressed directly. Indeed, when they are engaged as capable soldiers they have a lot to say about their experiences and the things they need to reestablish meaningful self-images.

As it stands, our mental-health approaches to veterans seem to reinforce their views of themselves as broken and useless in direct contradiction to former specialness. Wounded pride can be an unforgiving master.

Child and developmental psychologists remind us that childhood narcissism is a predictable and essential aspect of early attachment experiences. It is inextricably interwoven with the development of self-worth and identity. Through sounds, sights, and interactions, we create a personal world that reinforces our worth and relevance. In the interests of self-survival, we must put ourselves first. We must be of primary value to overcome the anxieties of living in a physical body that requires food, shelter, and protection from all sorts of threats to our existence.

Within our families, peer groups, and other social groups, however, we must learn to tailor our self-interest by not publicly putting ourselves before everybody else. As parents, we teach our children to share, to think of siblings and young friends, and to not be selfish. We often see the not-so-pleasant aspects of self-centeredness and invincibility among teens and young adults. Like the rest of us, young adults must believe that they matter and that the things they do matter—that they have agency to manipulate their environments in meaningful ways.

Normal development requires children to learn to modify self-centeredness and self-importance to get along with everybody else. Otherwise, they risk drawing the attention and possible wrath of others who necessarily must also believe that they are the center of the universe. There are daily examples of perceived attacks on people's specialness such as the oft-cited examples of road rage seemingly precipitated by a lack of respect from some presumed offender: "That self-centered prick cut me off intentionally...I am going to teach him a lesson!"

For those who enter military and first-response roles, special-ness once again becomes a central focus. They must demonstrate to other members of their respective "packs" assuredness in their abilities—confidence with a smidge of cockiness, but they must not be too arrogant to take instruction. They must learn to do two things simultaneously: hide any doubts about their abilities and keep secret beliefs in being above everyone else to themselves. The compromise is to display specialness through extraordinary deeds and competition with others, but the secret belief of being better than others must never be brandished publicly. Paradoxically, it is acceptable for others to bestow special recognition on them, though the recognition must be received with an appropriate de-gree of humility: "I didn't really deserve the honor. I was only do-ing my job." The inconsistency of the secret desire to be a hero combined with public displays of humility seems to occupy many of the first responders I know. Becker understands this paradox in terms of the search for personal meaning: "Man will lay down his life for his country, his society, his family. He will choose to throw himself on a grenade to save his comrades; he is capable of the highest generosity and self-sacrifice. But he has to feel and be-lieve that what he is doing is truly heroic, timeless, and supremely meaningful" (Becker, 6).

In a sense, narcissism among adults can be understood as a defense against fears of failure and lack of relevance. It is essential in helping us to avoid despair and simply giving up participating in life. However, among first responders of all types, the risk of narcissistic interest running amok can create real threats to the group through open conflict, abuses of authority, and interper-sonal aggression. Institutions that run on adrenaline are keenly aware of this problem; they have created strict containment strate-gies honed over generations. One of the primary strategies is the requirement for strong affiliation and subservience to the interests and espoused values of the group—the group is special. This specialness can be shared with a member by other members with the authority or the credibility to do so. Those members appearing to be too self-absorbed or too big for their britches are often identified and quickly cut down to size. This works to resolve the possibility of open rivalries, even though friendly competitiveness between members is encouraged to reinforce the qualities and behaviors that best serve the group's identity. For those individuals who do not rise to the challenge of contributing to the needs and standards of the group in meaningful ways, their membership can be quite tenuous—they are often ousted for lack of motivation and not being team players.

A central problem for soldiers is that the requirement to defer to the group as their primary source of psychological security and legitimacy can leave them vulnerable to profound disorientation when they leave. The personas they take on within these groups often have no place in general society. Many veterans report feeling as if they leave an essential part of themselves behind at the end of their careers. They risk being overwhelmed by an incomplete identity and invisibility as they are handed full responsibility for themselves. This is further complicated by the experience of separateness and loneliness. I believe that this is a serious dilemma for military veterans—the double edge of freedom from the group. My experience and observation is that the very psychological processes used to establish group identity can turn into a type of straightjacket that must be transcended if veterans are to move into genuine life and reasonable expressions of masculinity or femininity.

The experience of incomplete identity often requires former first responders to consider once again submitting to something beyond themselves to find relevance and reconnection to avoid shrinking into despair. Many of them gravitate to other first-response roles. For others, renewed relevance can come from deciding to be an emotionally engaged husband, father, community member, or volunteer, but it also means coming to terms with the loss of the persona they honed and portrayed in their former roles.

Many former soldiers talk about the desire to give back to others, which seems loosely reminiscent of Erik Erikson's notion of generativity—a desire to contribute to general society and the next generation versus stagnating and shrinking into self-absorption.[xxxiii] Many veterans occupy themselves with important causes—often in the service of others—but once again in somewhat detached sheepdog roles, which can be either good or bad for their overall mental health. Other military veterans, however—especially those discharged medically—can drift into self-absorbed cynicism and mistrust and continue to go it alone.

We cannot avoid discussing concepts like narcissism and egoism when we envision people convinced that they are special compared to everybody else. The notion of ego, linked closely with the work of Sigmund Freud, has lost its conceptual roots in everyday language. Even so, people who bluster and show an inflated sense of self-worth are often perceived as having big egos; they are egocentric or self-serving. Conversely, people who seem overly sensitive to minor criticisms are often described as having a fragile ego. A strong ego is also related to the notion of resiliency, which has spawned a cottage industry focused on helping first responders better manage the demands of their occupations. This notion of resiliency is not well operationalized; instead, it seems to be loosely understood to represent a person's ability to bounce back or even thrive in the face of adversity. The exact personal traits or prior life experiences that contribute to or erode resiliency have not been well articulated. Furthermore, it is interesting that while we talk about the need for resilient individuals, there is not much discussion of the characteristics of resilient organizations. If institutions and their leaders do not demonstrate their own capacity for honest self-reflection and maybe even humility, it seems unfathomable that individual members would be able to do this on their own.

For Erikson, basic trust is the fundamental attribute for personal resiliency to stress—those who are paranoid tend to fragment under strain, whereas those high in interpersonal trust seem to maintain optimal functioning.[xxxiv] Erikson based these observations on his work with American service personnel following World War II, noting that soldiers seemed to be worn down primarily through a million annoyances during their service:

> Above all, they felt that they did not know any more who they were: there was a distinct loss of ego identity. The sense of sameness and continuity and the belief in one's social role were gone. Furthermore, even among those who thrived in the military in highly specialized units seemed to break down after discharge because the war had provoked them into more ambitious self-images than their peacetime identities could afford to sustain. (p. 67)

Erikson's commentary continues to be a fitting description of the dilemmas facing our modern-day military veterans. They grapple with diminishment. They, too, are the products of our hero-making societal machinery that has no room for former heroes. We all have a part in convincing them that they were part of something special, part of history, part of traditions. Many of our veterans lose basic trust and come to believe that neither they nor the military were special. In effect, they realize that they may have been handed an empty set of promises from everyone in their lives. It will be incredibly challenging to confront these myths about specialness and invincibility in our military and first-responder institutions without tampering with family traditions steeped in our national narrative.

I wonder whether worn-out men and women—the special ones—present us with a malady that must be banished from our everyday awareness. We do not want to think that our incessant need to create and to worship temporary heroes of all sorts serves as a vital strategy to quell our shared anxieties over possible irrelevance and meaninglessness. Heroes are needed as social beacons to point a spotlight on our prized values; it even allows some people to live vicariously and to share in the successes of their chosen heroes. But we can't be honest about the fact that men and women in uniform, and others, like famous musicians, actors, and athletes, are all consumable and replaceable distractions. I suppose it must be this way in a seemingly fragmented society. Even so, every hero must believe that he is the best hero who has ever been and that he is essential and adored—this is the seduction of hero making. I see daily the effects of this fostered specialness among first responders, and I watch their declines when it comes to an end.

Six

Too Much to Handle

A squirrel scampers from the underbrush and springs onto a tree branch, nearly landing on the rope and straining in the morning breeze. Its rhythmic, mesmerizing song fills the stillness: Narrrrr—narrrrr—narrrrr. It is late spring, and a snow flurry is passing through, dropping big flakes on shoes straining toward the earth as if they would suddenly begin tiptoeing through the snow. But Danica Ristovsky will hang here alone for another eight days before being cut down and laid on the ground.

This has been Sarah's nightly movie for the past decade. Corporal Sarah Cote served as a member of the RCMP for fourteen years before being medically discharged. She tells me that the death of Danica was the final straw that broke her: "I just remember being handed a file that Easter Monday to investigate a missing nineteen-year-old female exchange student." Sarah knew her way around investigations and knew the criminal code inside out, to the chagrin of her male "cowboy" counterparts. She spoke with the missing girl's family, read her diary, talked with her few friends and roommates, and made copious notes about the young woman's routines and state of mind. She told me:

I didn't miss anything. I had this feeling in my gut that something terrible had happened, and I also had an idea of where she might be. When I asked the sergeant for a dog and a handler to start a search, he just told me to forget it and move on; I had already wasted too much time on a non-active file. So, I was sent on a road trip to deliver a bad guy to court. I was gone for about three days and heard about it on the radio as I was driving back to the detachment. A hunter had discovered a young woman's remains in a wooded area about a kilometer from the university campus. Almost exactly where I thought she might be. From there, it just went downhill for me. I can't forget her, and I can't forgive myself for not being there for her.

Sarah was supposed to be a boy; her father never let her forget this fact from the time she was little. Her dad was a successful businessman. In her memory, he was the stereotypical respected, church-going, community-minded family man known for his shrewdness and matter-of-fact attitudes about politics, business, and the place of the church in French culture. Her mom never worked outside the home, mostly because of her father's concern about how it would affect his reputation. Sarah tells me about her efforts to gain his attention—reading about business and engaging in discussions with him as a teenager and being physically active and outgoing to avoid ever being mistaken as just another silly girl. She even started a business degree at university but left to join the RCMP. She tells me that she was not shocked or even hurt by her father's reaction: "Why would you do that? You are taking a job away from a man." By this time, Sarah had expected nothing less, but she holds back from calling him chauvinistic. She still wanted to make him proud.

Sarah was content to live by her own morals and the sense of right and wrong she had learned from the nuns and from her father. She would be an ethical and fair Mountie, and she would help people in need—it felt like a calling to her. These beliefs sustained her through Depot, but she tells me that her first posting was an entirely different matter: "I ran into an RCMP version of my father who never even tried to hide his contempt for women in uniform. I worked for everything I got, from wrestling drunks even when I was pregnant with my son to taking the hard files just to prove to them that I was a good Mountie. But it never stopped. After Danica, I had nothing left." When Sarah told me this, she paused and looked at me squarely: "You know I broke every speeding law to get there before they cut her down? When I saw those damn rosary beads clasped in her hand, I knew I was done...Was anyone...Was God even listening to her last prayer?"

Like Corporal Cote, I was raised in the Catholic faith, attended a middle school run by Christian Brothers and was later taught by Jesuits in high school. By the time I joined the military, I already had a deeply rooted understanding of the values of humility, intellectual curiosity, and other qualities necessary to be a good person. I had also worked from the age of fifteen in heavy construction with other men—many of whom were rugged former miners. I was tested with increasing responsibilities to prove myself, and I gained their respect. It was a way of being with other men that I knew well before joining the military. And I had also been introduced to the importance of emotional toughness and aggression at an early age to protect myself from bullying—I learned to strike first. Paradoxically, I think these things buffered me from taking too seriously the military's version of manhood in the form of screaming NCOs and gruff senior leaders. Other younger kids were less fortunate, I believe.

For many teenagers, these big military personalities represent their first exposure to men in adult roles; these older men often come to serve as surrogates for their biological parents. The military had an entirely different idea about manhood; it was a kind of superficial identity based in pride, bravado, competition, and even arrogance. I understood just like everyone else the requirement to keep aggression in check just beneath the surface and to masquerade and simply fake the rest.

I was also taught that things like pride, greed, and envy constituted cardinal sins. These things had to be avoided because they led to immoral behavior. Today, these notions seem outdated in secular society, but they remain enshrined in our legal system and institutions like the military. And I believe that they are hidden within accepted treatments for trauma through references to resolving guilt, shame, remorse, confessing one's sins to another, seeking forgiveness, or engaging in acts of penance and repair— all religious leftovers. Indeed, over the years many critics have argued that the rise of the mental-health professionals has essentially served as a replacement for the role of religious leaders.

We should not forget that the clergy have always had a central place in war, and they continue to be a required element of the Canadian military. The padre is still considered to be the confidante and spiritual mentor for service personnel. And while good soldiers aspire to virtuous codes and values, the central activity of these warriors—killing—continues to be a source of moral dilemma for soldiers and indeed for the Canadian public. Having God on one's side provides the needed legitimacy and moral authority in war.

Fundamental disagreements over the morality of killing may explain the instinct within the military and among various political leaders to avoid acknowledging killing as a part of war. Indeed, for David Grossman,[xxxv] there seems to be a "massive unconscious cover-up" in which society hides itself from the true nature of combat. Even in the psychological and psychiatric literature on war, there is a kind of madness at work. Repugnance toward killing and the refusal to kill are referred to as acute combat reactions. And psychological trauma resulting from "slaughter and atrocity [is] called stress, as if the clinicians are talking about an executive's overwork." Grossman is a former soldier and psychologist and contends that neither the psychiatric or psychological literature offers a glimpse into the real horrors of war and its effect on those who fight it. He is quite clear in stating that this is not a military cover-up; instead, it is a shared "conspiracy of silence," a cultural conspiracy of forgetfulness, distortion, and lies that has been going on for millennia.

Within the inner sanctum of the military institution, lessons from previous wars have been translated into mental conditioning practices designed to push soldiers beyond their hesitancy to kill other people. Hoge outlined how this reluctance must be overcome by mastering the body and the mind of the soldier. Instilling a mental attitude of tenacity and aggression and a disregard for the humanness of enemies, supported by strategies like cognitive rehearsal and tactical breathing, serves to control biological processes. The ability to switch off conflicting moral values is essential. Soldiers who adhere too strongly to conflicting personal values represent a threat on the battlefield. It is essential that they give themselves over to the morality of the group—for better or worse in these situations. The act and the art of killing necessitates the creation and amplification of antisocial and other unvirtuous values; among these are things like unquestioning loyalty to the group, pride, and the belief in specialness of purpose. I must say that I have seen very few people who seemed to enjoy killing—those people devoid of empathy or compassion for other human beings who would likely be classified as psychopathic or sociopathic. Indeed, these people raise very troubling questions about human nature.

In the past several years, academic researchers and writers like Ledoux,[xxxvi] Lieberman,[xxxvii] Porges,[xxxviii] and Davidson and Begley[xxxix] have argued convincingly that neurobiological explanations of PTSD and other mental-health problems are inadequate because they are based on incorrect assumptions about the role of structural damage to key brain regions. Instead, their combined research efforts indicate that the entire emotional life of the human organism and life experiences must be incorporated into our understanding of all mental-health functions. In fact, all types of mental distress are usually whole brain experiences that are not genetically predetermined. There is a convincing argument to be made that behaviors and neurological changes associated with mental illness may simply reflect epigenetic changes resulting from adaptations to one's social environment.

Mentally distressed military personnel and other first responders, however, continue to be taught a language that carries considerable medical baggage. They learn that anything upsetting emotionally is to be labeled as a trigger conceptualized within a loose theory that their brains have gone offline temporarily requiring them to downregulate through specific mental exercises, medications, or social withdrawal. This is good advice to manage oneself during an emotional crisis. After all, as it stands, medical diagnoses are the only authority clinicians currently have at their disposal to offer formal help. But nowhere does this advice provide real opportunities for these men and women to reengage socially or develop their self-reflective capacities to determine the complexity of emotions and conflicted value systems that may have been brought to the forefront. This medicalized approach to trauma literally guarantees a continuing cycle of being ramped up, calming oneself down, and doing it all over again endlessly. As it is constructed, there is often no way forward. Likewise, there are no explanations for those who recover completely (e.g., the possibility that one's amygdala or emotional centers have been re-paired). Unsurprisingly, there is considerable disagreement as to whether a person can ever truly recover from things like PTSD or depression or whether these problems simply go into a remissive state like cancer or addiction to alcohol.

I advanced the position in *Ghost on the Ranks*[xl] that the require-ment of uniformity within the group forces military members to separate or to compartmentalize their internal thoughts and emotions and keep them from interfering with the overall goals of training. One's private world is necessarily traded, maybe even rejected, in the interest of adopting a common military identity—an identity referred to as the *reconstituted collective self.* To recap briefly, this term refers to the argument that a military person's sense of self becomes conditioned to the beliefs, values, and needs of the larger group, which requires separation from the internal life. Subservience to the group and to the authority of commands are both the goals and the outcomes of successful military social-ization and conditioning. It can be argued, then, that each soldier is the personification of the group's identity. In many cases, he does not have a complete sense of identity apart from the group. This is exemplified in a remark like this: "When I left the military, it was like part of me was missing...I can't explain it." So, when we consider the effects of a traumatic event for a particular soldier, we might also consider that it represents a group trauma, since each member is the group and vice versa. In fact, I don't think that we can talk about an affected member without considering the group. The ways in which the group manages its losses and grievances, how it manages frustrations over ROEs and orders, the things it does to reconstitute its pride and morale, and the ways in which it reacts in the aftermath of serious events can be seen through the varied reactions of specific members and the interactional patterns within the group. The section or unit may regress into silence and antagonism or, conversely, members of the unit may become more engaged with one another. This need for groups to reconstitute and repair themselves may offer a partial explanation for the reported successes of informal debriefings, critical incident stress groups, social media subgroups, and even homogeneous group sessions with first-responders and military veterans. These fora can provide the possibility for groups to reconnect and reconstitute themselves and by default also help individual members. Again, I think it is unreasonable to single out specific members as broken—not us—and expect them to resolve the group's trauma on their own.

Seven

If There Is No God, I Must Be It

Jack had decided to continue working as a contractor for the military since retiring five years ago. His expertise in military strategy and tactics and hand-to-hand combat skills were still valuable. He had spent a thirty-year career in the army with multiple deployments to Bosnia, Afghanistan, and other places that he could not tell me about. He told me that his career had been littered with consequences—a serious problem with alcohol that he addressed after the end of his first marriage and several suicide attempts in the past couple of years, but he had to keep going. "I don't want to think about any of that stuff, the things we did… the stuff I have done and seen. The guys I was with are the only ones who would understand." Likewise, he was not interested in providing details other than snippets about the beatings from his father growing up and being locked in a closet for days at a time without food or water. "None of that stuff matters to me. He's dead, and it's all history. I just need to keep moving ahead and find a good reason not to kill myself."

Pride in one's abilities to switch into an automaton mode is believed by many to protect soldiers from the visceral effects of witnessing and causing suffering and death. As has been established, soldiers must believe that they are special people, with special abilities, and with the moral authority to engage in terrible acts if necessary. Efforts to assist those people left to reconcile the aftereffects of violence often sanitize soldiers' experiences and reactions under the heading of symptoms, focusing on possible failings in their thinking or attitudes and ultimately convincing them to forget about the past. Nobody seems interested in discussing the consequences of mental conditioning for armed conflict—it is simply an accepted aspect of the institution and our national narrative. This means that when soldiers leave the military, all their training in aggression and special identity must be forgotten as if it never existed. Many veterans report having lost their "switch" to control aggression in day-to-day life that they find intolerable and mundane. Very often their safest strategies are social avoidance and silence. Importantly, this silence keeps from the public the direct experiences of soldiers who witness actual events on the ground, some of which could be less than flattering to the image of the military and our political leaders. A veteran who had been active in Bosnia told me, "We were told that we were there to help people, but all we did was watch and do nothing. We were warned to keep our mouths shut when we got home."

Canadian soldiers have seen and done things and have been convinced that they form part of a special collective of men and women reshaped from who they were before joining the military. Training designed to toughen them and to hone specific personal characteristics and abilities leads to acceptance within this special society. Weakness and vulnerability are banished and replaced by a persona hinging on invincibility and assuredness. These young men and women are gradually transformed into larger-than-life versions of themselves with the skills, equipment, and authority to kill and destroy on behalf of Canadians. I have chosen the term *specialness* to describe this transformation, but I believe it hardly gives enough credit to the impact of these manufactured personas on the minds of former youngsters. These contrived and yet essential personas form the essence of the military's raison d'être.

If these attributes come to form core aspects of personality structures, then, I believe that postservice declines like social isolation, addiction, and premature deaths must also be understood as an aspect of the loss of this shared identity and the absence of a replacement. I believe that their conditioning and experiences in uniform risk separating them from everyday people when they leave the military. Now, five years after the official end of Canada's involvement in the Afghanistan War, an unending cadre of men and women who served there continue to exit the military for medical reasons. These younger men and women are not interested in relinquishing their recently acquired larger-than-life personas—many of them continue to seek all-encompassing outlets to recreate the sensation of feeling fully alive.

And there is also a tragic downside—those who fall into despair and decide to end their lives. This uncomfortable reality has gone virtually unnoticed by most media outlets and the public. In recent years, the risk of suicide appears to be highest among young male soldiers and veterans.[xli,xlii] Average Canadians are unaware of this situation for the most part. Indeed, there has been an insistence through public statements cautioning that reporting these suicides could contribute to contagion and copycat suicides. I am unaware of the research into this phenomenon among military veterans in Canada. While responsible, nonsensationalized reporting is certainly required, calls for a wholesale blackout of information may simply reflect a public relations problem for politicians and the military. It may also be a leftover from the days when we believed that broaching the topic of suicide with clients might somehow put the idea in their heads, as if they had not considered it previously.

Officially, Canada releases about ten thousand personnel annually. According to a recent government report, approximately 16 percent of them are released for medical reasons. [xliii] Despite the many programming initiatives aimed at veterans, the rates of difficult transitions to civilian life appear to be trending upward; they were estimated at 25 percent in 2011 and were up to 32 percent in 2016. [xliv,xlv] This increase has been attributed to the aftereffects of Afghanistan, where nearly 40 percent of medical releases are among soldiers with less than ten years of service from the lower ranks. I can't help but worry about the life trajectories for these young men and women. I think we must wonder about the disconnect they are experiencing between societal and military cultural values that may contribute to a lifetime of lingering problems.

The consequences of conditioning under the Spartan notion of the soldier-warrior will be incredibly difficult to leave behind. Our shared British preoccupation with public image and the importance of emotional suppression—stiff upper lip and keeping one's private lives to oneself in the interests of public image cannot be ignored either. Our Western allies experience these same problems in their newly minted veterans. Veteran support in the form of financial compensation, education and retraining, and transitional programming continues to be debated in the wake of physical injuries, premature deaths, and other personal tragedies among young veterans.

It is striking and disappointing that governments seem incapable of responding amid secret deliberations and decisions: "Well, they were volunteers, weren't they? Nobody forced them to join. They knew what they were signing up for, and we didn't ask them to go over there." These cavalier attitudes among some serving and retired military people and civilians alike attest to our ongoing ambivalence about the notion of operational-stress injuries in the military. Since we are protected from the realities of war zones, most people are not quite sure what all the fuss is about. So, maybe we owe them nothing; maybe they are just faking or looking for attention or a free ride! Fortunately, this stance although significant remains a barely audible undercurrent because it is simply unacceptable to parents and communities who have lost children to the latest mission and to those among us who know firsthand the devastation experienced by these men and women.

The public seems to believe strongly that government officials—but not individual citizens—have responsibilities in taking care of these war heroes-turned nomads who show up in their communities. And, from a public relations standpoint, we can never forget that there is always a need for youngsters to replace the worn-out ones, so politicians and the DND (Department of National Defence) public relations machinery have little choice but to present the military as a larger-than-life, yet benevolent and caring organization. It is no secret that our military is facing a recruiting crisis; a massive campaign is under way to attract minorities, women, indigenous and immigrant groups, and sexually diverse populations to fill the gaps left behind by the absence of its traditional base—young white males who often came from challenged backgrounds. These changes are expected and necessary. I think the real challenge facing our military will come down to its interest and ability to pivot away from traditional military conditioning rituals and ethos to reflect people who have not been exposed to the tenets of accepted masculinity—pride, bravado, self-importance, and self-reliance. There are many who will view such changes negatively—feminization of the military—but the reality is that recruiting shifts will likely create incredible strains on the continuing reliance on the Spartan warrior mentality.

These new efforts seem to be occurring in an environment where we are also experiencing a resurgence of a phenomenon that was present in Canada after World War I. Veterans are speaking publicly about inadequate care and the betrayal of political promises, and even advising young Canadians to not join the military until these matters are resolved—a drastic step since veterans usually remain quite loyal to the military institution despite their own grievances.

When it comes to our government's contribution to these issues, I don't think we can ignore the repercussions from its preemptive strike in the late 1980s with the invocation of a Universality of Service (U of S) doctrine. It enshrined the cardinal need for uniformity—that any soldier must be replaceable instantly by an equally capable person. U of S effectively castrated the impending Human Rights Legislation, which would hold employers, including the military, accountable through a requirement of a duty to accommodate. The consequence of this action continues to reverberate throughout Canada's military and veteran communities, especially among the medically released. In fairness, the military hierarchy could not have foreseen the ramifications of this decision and likely had little choice to ensure an effective fighting force given the persistent struggles for adequate funding and resources. This shift was also likely due to a lack of interest among the generals of that time to consider making room for the "sick, lame, and lazy" among its ranks. During the writing of this book, the current federal government has given signals of its intention to relax strict U of S requirements on a case-by-case basis. Initial reactions from the veteran community have been somewhat mixed, but a majority seem to see this shift as a long overdue change in policy. We should also not forget the federal government's decision in 2006 to eliminate lifelong care and financial support to military veterans. This change has created an open conflict between military veterans and our political leaders. It fuels a morale-destroying belief among serving members and veterans that their service to the country means little, despite the oft-cited cliché of a grateful nation.

Men and women who are trained and familiar with controlled aggression and lethality are essential in the conduct of war, and there is no way to soften this reality. This warrior mentality has also served beyond identified battlefields (e.g., the Oka Crises of the early 1990s, disasters in Haiti, training missions in Ukraine, and the invocation of Canada's War Measures Act) and domestic emergencies (e.g., the Swiss Air disaster, devastating wildfires, search and rescue missions, floods, and other national disasters) requiring the same tough mental skill set, albeit to a lesser degree. The challenge for many military veterans as they reenter civilian life is first to contend with the separation from this adopted culture and second to begin the difficult work of reconciling their experiences, which in some cases means rebuilding themselves. This often means reconciling the loss of their previous identities.

In his book *Tribe*, Sebastian Junger[xlvi] provides an insightful account of the intimate bonds that the war experience creates among military personnel and the profound loss they experience when they return home to isolation and disconnection. I would add another element to his main point—namely, that military people also reminisce about deployments because of a desire to recapture the clarity of purpose and the nostalgic image of who they were during those times. They miss the personal sense of what it felt like to be fully alive and special. A veteran of Afghanistan said to me, "Man, we were fuckin' rock stars over there…Celebrities, dignitaries, and even politicians showing up in a war zone to play ball hockey, thanking us, shaking our hands."

Once released, these former soldiers often find themselves in a mundane and nebulous world—civil society—devoid of clear-cut rules and with other people who seem to anonymously conduct their predictable lives. Many of them tell me that their lack of ability to fit into this world was an important reason for joining the military in the first place. Now, they must contend again with a world that is simply not big enough to fulfill inflated ego requirements. Some can continue in these larger-than-life roles by shifting into other first-response organizations, while many others join or create fringe groups to fulfill these needs. Many of the people I see have moved to take on special projects in the service of veterans and other causes; they are uninterested in just getting a job like average people. They realize that the term *society* ends up as nothing more than an empty abstraction unless they can find places to meet self-worth needs. From the outside, it is difficult to locate; it exists everywhere and nowhere at the same time. Military veterans can experience a fundamental disconnect between their engrained military value system and those required of them as they reenter civil society. At the top of the list is a struggle to contend with invisibility, lack of relevance, and the loss of special attention of any sort in this world; the skills of hyperfocus, emotional suppression, and prepared alertness have few places of value.

Over the years, I have come to know many veterans who have taken on special causes and projects—all very important in their own right—to fill the void left from lost specialness. They are committed to these causes, sometimes at the cost of their physical and mental health and their family relationships. As I see it, these projects serve to help many of them to contend with emptiness and dislocation—the disruption of their established sense of control and relevance.

Eight

No Room for Vulnerability

"If you can fix the problems with my back, Doc, then I am all ears. Otherwise I can't see any reason to talk to a shrink." Steve was a good-looking monster of a man—broad shouldered, with massive tattooed arms and a slim waist. He was in his early forties and stood about six feet two inches tall. He wore combat pants, military style boots, and a T-shirt with *Afghanistan* stenciled on the back. He was told to come to see me because of a drinking episode that landed him in the hospital. "Eight to ten beers a day plus my weed keeps the pain under control and helps me sleep. It's better than all the pills they tried to shove down my throat…My way keeps me calm enough so I don't rip the throat out of stupid people."

Steve told me that he had been drinking when the right side of his face went numb with a pronounced droop. "I didn't care, but my wife freaked and was determined to call the ambulance, which landed me in hospital. So, here I am." He became visibly upset as he told me about his fear of losing his physical shape and that despite his leg injury he continued to weight train nearly every day:

I can't accept that I am turning into a cripple. I can't stand being around people. Traffic drives me nuts, especially in the city. I immediately switch back to driving in the convoys, and I just want to hit the gas and plow through traffic. I got rid of Facebook, and I stay away from all the whiners...I punched out one of them at the tavern because he wouldn't shut his trap, so now I am banned from there... Ya know, when I got back from 'Stan, because of my leg problems they sent me to the base hospital and to the social worker. My warrant officer thought I was too aggressive. Imagine that! She asked me about the tour, so I told her what I thought she wanted to hear and got out of there as fast as I could. Out of nowhere, I'm on medical restrictions and the RSM [regimental sergeant major] calls me in to basically tell me that I was losing my section to ride a desk. I walked out, got in my car, and drove from Ontario straight back home to the Prairies. It's funny...I was home for three months before anyone called me.

Steve stopped talking briefly, took a sip of his coffee, smiled at me, and continued:

So, I get this call from the RSM... He tells me to get my ass back to Ontario or I'll be charged for absent without leave. I tell him that unless he's gonna give me back my job, I wasn't going anywhere. So, he starts off warning me that the military police would be showing up to arrest me. I lost it and told him that he could send whoever he wanted, but he'd better send a fuckin' bunch of them because people were gonna get hurt...Just slammed the phone down on him. That was it, never heard another word until about nine months later…I get this envelope in the mail telling me that I was medically released. The reason they gave was failure to meet universality because of my leg and because of mental-health issues. So, fuck 'em anyway…Never even went back to clear my shit out.

Steve stared off as if watching something in the distance and stopped talking. The silence gave me time to focus on comments in his medical file: "Steve, says here that they thought you might have PTSD because of—"

He cut me off midsentence:

You know what I think…all this PTSD talk is just a pile of bullshit to keep the whiners happy. These people should never have been allowed to put on a fuckin' uniform in the first place. As far I'm concerned, when the military started scraping the bottom of the barrel for more boots on the ground and allowed those liberal bleeding hearts to dictate policy, we started going downhill. Nothing but a bunch of momma's boys who want to run and hide under a rock if they see something or if they get their "f-e-e-l-i-n-g-s" hurt! Jesus, makes me sick hearing about all this bullshit.

This man easily meets the criteria for PTSD, but he will never accept such a diagnosis. He's an extremely proud man who had built a reputation as a straightforward, in-your-face soldier who made no apologies to anyone and always said what needed to be said. He has no interest in changing anything, including his continued search for aggressive outlets. Steve is representative of other soldiers who find themselves under the OSI umbrella following deployments. While they may quietly struggle to reconcile their deployments, pride and ego means that they would never lower themselves to ask for or accept help from anybody. Instead, they often double down on self-containment and an aggressive stand when they sense that things are slipping out of their control.

Irrespective of mental diagnoses, soldiers like Steve seem to exist in a personality type somewhere between the stories of Adonis and Narcissus. They have the perfect male body but are completely absorbed in the image of their own physical appearance. There are many of them in the military, but they are also well represented in professional sport and other institutions that encourage physical prowess. In fact, the phenomenon even has a name—the Adonis complex.[xlvii] These men, and some women for that matter, are preoccupied with physical attractiveness, virility, and being bigger and physically stronger than anybody else as the epitome of true masculinity. The alternative to this level of preoccupation with prowess, of course, is not some form of emasculated vulnerable male. Either extreme seems to reduce people to one-dimensional distortions—there are times and places where independence and aggressive action are appropriate, and there are also times when paying attention to qualities like compassion and humility are appropriate.

Irreverence, pride, and even cynicism masked by polite diplomacy characterize common traits among many soldiers. Other less attractive traits like determined obstinacy and vanity can also exist under the umbrella of pride. Young men and women are turned into soldiers and transformed through lessons in loyalty, sacrifice, professionalism, rules, and a paradoxical yet required mix of other qualities like sociopathy, competitiveness, ethics and morality, aggression, and self-pride bordering on narcissism.

These contradictions can create an incredible internal conflict for military members. People tell me that it is like being two different people—the mask that is displayed publicly in uniform and the private one that must be kept secret at all costs. The experience of flipping back and forth can be extremely tiring and confusing. Soldiers' investments in their external roles and reputations often work very well in keeping their private worlds in check. Upon retirement, however, unless they find replacements in other first-response roles or things like extreme sports, there is often no outlet for many of these qualities. Their internal worlds can seem to flood in upon them, especially when their adopted military persona fails to solve problems.

Younger veterans sometimes yearn for the "dysfunctional family" where straightforward interactions, physicality, extreme behavior, and high adrenaline roles are the norm. They describe contending with the absence of outlets to unleash their unbridled selves—the one that is driven by pride and adrenaline. Experiences of dramatic, over-the-top interactions and activities serve as readily available discharges for anything they may be contending with emotionally. Again, I think about Erikson's observations that the outside world is often too small to fulfill the ego needs of these young men and women. The other possibility of considering their private worlds—whether it is the experience of devastation, sadness, or regrets—comes with incredible self-judgment and the instinct to suppress these things. Here's a story to highlight this phenomenon: Early in my career—before Canada's official recognition of military trauma—I saw a soldier who had been diagnosed with alcohol dependence because of an altercation with his sergeant after returning from Bosnia. This man drank only twice a year, but during these three-day binges he would get into all sorts of trouble—domestic violence, destroying property, and getting into fights that often landed him in court. While he technically met official criteria for an alcohol problem, the diagnosis missed the point entirely. He described a life in the military of being a hard worker and passively putting up with things, effectively suppressing and ignoring the things he could not deal with and then letting go of all self-restraint during these binges. These major discharges helped him manage his life—for better and worse. As stated by Hoge, PTSD does not account for many of the strains facing returning soldiers:

> Society believes that a warrior should be able to transition home and lead a "normal" life, but the reality is that most of society has no clue what it means to be a warrior. Those who have worked in a war zone understand that their warrior responses—including responses doctors may label "PTSD"—could be needed again in the future—for instance, if they mobilize for another deployment, someone tries to break into their home, or they take a job in a dangerous profession (e.g., law enforcement, security, emergency services). (Hoge, xii)

Hoge argued that the majority of those who participate in war zones, even after facing extreme stress and trauma, do not develop PTSD. Research in Canada has highlighted similar findings; however, they are also not the same person after deployment who they were before. They react differently after deployment. There is often a strength of character that is sharp and direct, but one that may make family members and even other people in the military feel uncomfortable. There is maturity, but combat also takes its toll and can make them feel older. Warriors are more independent, but this may also make it more difficult for them to tolerate authority at work or "stupid" conflicts within their personal relationships. Their experiences transform them into people who do not fit into general society. Up to now, we have not been interested in making room for them. This outcome seems tragically ironic to me: the very society they were protecting has no room for them. Many veterans report having a hard time reconnecting with loved ones, despite their demonstrated ability to form lifelong bonds with unit peers. This is not only because of how they've changed but also because family members and society don't necessarily understand these changes, or they view these changes as bad or as signs of mental illness. Unfortunately, PTSD has become confused with various normal reactions that veterans experience.

As a social behavior, emotional expression serves primarily for biological survival of our species by enabling connection with other people. In Western society, however, emotionality is often misunderstood and denigrated as self-indulgence and a sign of weak character. This seems to be particularly the case among traditional-minded white males who often hold onto the idea of rationality and rugged individualism as a sign of adulthood. Among this group, particularly in the United States, the rate of death among these males appears to be steadily rising because of drug overdoses, suicides, and alcohol-related liver disease—dubbed deaths of despair.[xlvii] The same trends have been found in Canada.[xlix] A host of reasons have been advanced to explain this phenomenon, including economic crises, alcohol and prescription overuse, and relationship breakdowns. These are all important factors, but we have yet to consider things like social dislocation and emotional isolation to explain this emerging phenomenon. Traditional masculinity centers on pragmatism and activity-driven connection to other people; emotional connection to others seems to occur primarily through humor or anger—male value hinges on doing things.

Males seem particularly good at creating pseudorelationships—those who exclude vulnerability and intimacy with other people, including spouses, friends, and children. Males have learned to be very good at hiding emotional struggles.

The safe expression of emotion serves to reestablish connection to other people. So, the real benefit for any trauma survivor is that when they do not have to expend all their energy in emotional avoidance or containment they have more mental energy to engage in their relationships and other areas of life. Unfortunately, emotions have been incorrectly portrayed as cauldrons of hidden energy and self-indulgence that interferes with a preferred state—stoic rationality. LeDoux's work, however, highlights that emotionality is nothing more than a component of a social signally system designed primarily to draw us closer to people. The implication of LeDoux's work is that we must learn to acknowledge and to communicate in emotional language just as we learn to engage in rational conversations. In fact, positive neurobiological effects have been detected via functional magnetic resonance imaging scans from the simple act of privately naming one's emotional states. The unhelpful misunderstanding that expressions of strong emotion signal some deep-rooted biological dysfunction must be overcome.

Let's face it: first responders love the adrenaline chase. Maybe, even in the interests of narcissistic fulfillment—it allows them to feel truly alive. These roles come with incredible boosts to self-worth and a sense of omnipotence. Humans thrive on the challenge; people chase it no matter the cost and then attempt to deal with any consequences later. Conditioning and training hones this, amplifies it, while interactions with peers reinforce and support it to get tough jobs done. I have worked with many first responders who describe themselves unapologetically as adrenaline junkies, always looking for new ways to charge up again—through anger, conflict, physical exercise, or volunteering for risky duties to feel alive. Many of them openly admit to being some of the strongest critics of other people who reported mental declines when they were in full operational modes. They had simply kept pushing until it all came crashing in.

Nine

It's a Metamorphosis, Not a Transition

Ya know, I've been out nearly two years. Marriage is on the rocks. My own brothers and sisters won't talk to me anymore...can't sleep...pissed off all the time, but I just smile at everyone on the outside. God damn it, I was the chief...I was the center; it was me that got things done. I loved the intensity and always having multiple things going on all at once. It used to piss me off when we had to go to the bunker for hours because of stupid rocket attacks over there. I even asked to have a desk set up there so I could continue working instead of wasting valuable time. I don't want to be out, I hate it out here, and if my body had not let me down physically, I would still be there.

—Afghanistan veteran

This soldier's dilemma fits under the general rubric of *transitional strain*. It is not a well-defined term. It seems to span the time from getting back home, completing postdeployment health assessments, going through a honeymoon period, taking block leave, undergoing more postdeployment health monitoring, spending a year or years back home, taking another possible deployment, possibly leaving the military for a new job, remustering to a new military occupation, contending with marital strains and possible separation/divorce, dealing with physical injuries, and facing the prospect of medical release. Likewise, there is no clear definition of a normal readjustment period, but the two years immediately following service seem to be particularly risky.

The ways in which soldiers and family members describe this experience often reflect a gap in perspectives. Married service members returning home often cannot comprehend anything worse than living constantly under threat, while their spouses often believe they had it worse—waiting, worrying, single-parenting, running the household alone, and juggling life at home. A reality for military families is that life can take them on different trajectories during these absences. Soldiers return home out of sync with normal life and sometimes find it overwhelming to contend with their children's difficulties, normal family stressors, and their own hyperaroused mental states.

Within the broader societal context, Canadians seem to be a bit confused, if not conveniently absentminded and oblivious, in their attitudes about maintaining a military force capable of lethality. The culture seems to be extremely uncomfortable with the realities of killing and collateral carnage associated with war, so it is kept out of public view with the help and the insistence of our political masters. I think it also belies an uncomfortable paradox about the culture. Canadians aspire to the image of being friendly, accommodating, and self-effacing people, but our national history tells another story—one replete with examples of aggression, indifference, and inhumanity toward our indigenous peoples.[l,li]

By denying violence, we mentally separate it from ourselves, secretly cheer on those who engage in the messiness of war on our behalf, and then disavow it publicly at the same time. In any event, the omission of the realities of war from public discourse leaves various governments free to downsize the military, increase its size incrementally when needed, fund it variously when embarrassed over antiquated equipment or personnel shortages, engage in secretive agonizing over where to send small contingents, deny and keep from the public the realities of death and destruction necessarily carried out by Canadian soldiers, and then drag their feet when called to extend support to those who are wounded or killed.

The image of the Canadian soldier is a carefully crafted national cliché that often has little in common with who these warriors are as men and women. Amid all the shuffling and hand wringing on the heels of the latest tragedy involving serving or retired members of the military, politicians deftly avoid acknowledgment of responsibility or legal obligation. Instead, they relegate these responsibilities to their bureaucrats for "issues management." I have come to understand this to be a strategy meant to aggressively target bad or embarrassing news and quickly remove it from the news cycle and from public scrutiny. In this sense then, the military is very much a political instrument to be guarded and employed judiciously. Politicians understand the value of appearing military friendly and seem content to continue their oversight roles as benevolent benefactors, like the feudal lords of old. The notion of the king's mercy is politically useful. Therefore, the arguably legal requirements and obligations to prepare these damaged men and women for meaningful lives after military service do not ever seem to be considered: after all, nobody asked them to join!

In my work over the years, I have met many sincere people sprinkled throughout the CAF generally and among the leadership who work tirelessly to improve the lives of military members and their families. I served with some of them and have come to know many others in veteran-support initiatives. While they have made progress over the decades, many of them are also eventually worn down by bureaucracy, or they run out of time because of mandatory retirements. They are often faced with the intransigence of a legalistic and myopic system preoccupied with its own processes and continued existence; I suppose that is the price to be paid for consistency and predictability.

As noted by various Ombudsmen for VAC and the CAF, the functioning and priorities of our Canadian military and veteran bureaucracies seem to be insulated from the influences of political will or public sentiment. Our elected men and women, no matter their official titles, seem to be tolerated and placated until they leave to be replaced by a new bunch of wide-eyed MPs to be educated about how things really work. As suggested pointedly by retired Colonel Pat Stogran in his recent book *Rude Awakening*,[lii] our public servants may be the real masters when it comes to decisions about responding to the ongoing needs of Canadian veterans. As reported publicly on many occasions in Canada over the past decade, disgruntled veterans were targeted as problems, their personal information was made public, and others were simply ignored because they raised thorny yet legitimate concerns.

An alternative to disavowing those who speak up seems to be to co-opt them when it is politically advantageous by sharing the credit for grassroots solutions that are supported publicly. In this sense, then, our bureaucrats would seem to be more political than politicians who believe they are in charge. This is predictable to some degree. Bureaucracies ensure continuity and predictability. When a culture combines them with public apathy and the absence of open debate, the culture ensures that existing arrangements continue despite incremental changes. For the most part, this conservative-minded tinkering does not often interfere with the Canadian way of conducting business as usual.

Since the early 1990s, veterans who served in multiple and overlapping missions have been separated into subpopulations. Many of them continue to vanish into the proverbial wind without the skills, supports, or realistic opportunities to contribute to their communities or their families. These *broken toys* (a term often used by medically released soldiers) seem to me to represent somewhat of an irritant to the military and Canadian society because they present us with a reality that is diametrically opposed to the accepted stereotype of Canadian soldiers. They cannot be acknowledged.

For the most part, the public is disengaged and excluded from discussions of proposed combat and military deployments. For all the sacrifices in support of the all-but-forgotten Afghanistan War, there were no spoils of war or victories to share and in fact most people did not even agree with our involvement. Maybe the nod of acceptance from our neighbors to the south mattered more to us than our opinion of ourselves. After all, it appears that we needed to redeem ourselves for passing on the war in Iraq.

In contrast to our allies, we usually do not acknowledge the heroics of our soldiers. By all accounts that I have heard and read, our elite snipers in Afghanistan did a superb job killing many people, but this dirty and grisly aspect of the war was kept away from the public. The US military's acknowledgments of our soldiers reportedly sparked investigations and ended in the essential removal of these men from the military.[53] So it seems that war is an honorable endeavor as long as our cherished national narrative remains intact. We are uncomfortable with the nasty business of war—it is unbecoming and embarrassing to recognize those people who kill on our behalf, placing it front and center. Veterans experience this paradox all the time; good soldiers are expected to be capable killing machines who cannot be acknowledged outside or even inside the military. Ambivalence over desired and deserved recognition plays itself out when soldiers denigrate their earned medals as "shiny trinkets" or poke fun at a peer who is nominated for doing something extraordinary. If the military could be honest about the exploits of its members, it would likely force Canadians to engage in an honest accounting of this country's true history and our complex and contradictory roles in the world. It would certainly provide veterans with a sense of relevance in the broader society.

Ten

Let the Dogs Loose

"They trained us to be killers: Kill! Kill! Kill! It just keeps going round and round in my head." These are the words of a veteran who served in Afghanistan. The Canadian Army's official ethos hinges on duty, integrity, honor, and discipline. Nowhere do we find words that describe the act or the art of killing. Instead, we employ other terms—*enforcing security, neutralizing enemies, succeeding in operations, maintaining unit cohesion, aiming for mission success,* and *responding to threat environments under the laws of armed conflict.* Multiple turns of phrase as shown in the following quote are designed to mask a central focus of conditioning and training—perfecting the organized killing of other people.

> The habits and predispositions that are instilled in a soldier are dictated by the events that are to be encountered. For example, for a soldier, often the events to be faced are fearful—thus habits are formed that enable fear to be coped with; and, the events to be faced may oblige the use of lethal force—thus habits are formed that enable lethal force

to be deployed upon lawful command. Habits are formed that affirm the proper use of the Chain of Command, as well as habits that generate discipline. All these habits, and more, are instilled through practice and repetition.[liv]

The role of any military and its leadership is to establish the conditions necessary to hone and then to control aggression, including the use of deadly force to be inflicted on sanctioned enemies. This reality and ultimate goal of military conditioning is so engrained and accepted that it is virtually invisible to all participants. It is only visible when aggression erupts inappropriately—through unsanctioned kills or acts of indecency enacted on one another in the game of dominance-submission, rank-based harassment, or physical and sexual violence. Sometimes aggression erupts on civilian spouses, family members, or everyday people outside the control or grasp of the military. The legacy of this acquired aggression cannot be talked about in these terms. And, when members and veterans turn their aggression on themselves, it must also be recast, normally as a sign of some unrecognized mental disease.

"Cry havoc and let slip the dogs of war." William Shakespeare's infamous line of dialogue continues to have relevance in the conditioning and roles of modern-day soldiers. As in all previous wars, there are specific codes of conduct, circumstances where killing is permitted, and decisions made by leaders of all types to let loose their charges. We have high-minded ideals—protecting the innocent or backing one another in battle—that support soldiers in overcoming the resistance to killing. But soldiers must also be introduced to something else, a mental place where life and death, including their own deaths, means less. They must be introduced to being dehumanized, which in turn allows them to view others—the enemies—as less than human. Words offer a very powerful way of providing emotional distance and even hatred toward others—*savages, gooks, slopes, skinnies, hodgies, dinks, chinks,* and *ruskies* to name a few. Dehumanizing terms are also used to describe women, minorities, and less-than-ideal soldiers—*groundsheets, rear echelon mother fuckers, numpties, shit-pumps,* and on and on it goes. These strategies have been perfected over hundreds of years and speak to the psychology of military conditioning—it is as much mental as it is physical training; we can't have one without the other.

The embodied ability to kill without hesitation upon command is an unspoken code of understanding between soldiers that is rarely acknowledged openly and not ever to civilians. It is implied through standard operating procedures and ROEs but never stated explicitly. Isn't it important enough to talk about? I think so. I am not saying that it is good or bad, just that this reality of war and armed conflict cannot continue to be sanitized out of our reality if we are to understand veteran distress. This shared silence over killing is certainly a problem for many who have carried out or witnessed these deeds on our behalf. I hear this repeatedly—usually when a youngster has been killed accidentally, or when a soldier has been confronted with starving or destitute people who could not be helped or defended or has witnessed collateral damage. If we can't discuss the underbelly of war and war-making institutions, then I don't think we can honestly say that we are committed to understanding military OSIs. Another quote to demonstrate how the realities of war and armed conflict are languaged away.

The military ethos embodies the spirit that binds the military profession together. It is a living spirit that finds its full expression through the conduct of members of the profession of arms. It clarifies how members view their responsibilities, apply their expertise, and how they express their unique military identity. It establishes an ethical framework for the professional conduct of all activities and military operations.

The uniquely Canadian military ethos is made up of three fundamental components: beliefs and expectations about military service; Canadian values; and Canadian military values. It affirms core notions of military service: unlimited liability, fighting spirit, discipline and teamwork. It reflects that the legitimacy of the profession of arms in Canada requires that it embody the same values and beliefs as the society it defends and that the values of the profession must be in harmony with the values of that society. It defines the subordination of the armed forces to civilian control and the rule of law. Finally, the ethos places a special emphasis on the Canadian military values of duty, loyalty, integrity, and courage.[lv]

When soldiers, particularly those from Afghanistan who represent a generation of still young men in their thirties, realize that they are not invincible, they begin to reevaluate their learned version of manhood and often discover a profound emptiness. An Afghan vet recently told me about the crushing effects of losing a bar fight with civilians several months after his return: "Everything went to shit after that for me; now I am anxious all the time. How could I, a hardened combat vet, be beaten by snot-nosed civvies? It was like I lost my edge and I can't get it back." This altercation seemed to undermine his confidence—erode his shield—so much so that a year and a half later he was exited from the military for chronic depression. Was this an OSI from Afghanistan surfacing or a by-product of his military training and value system? This is an essential question because I think we continue to confuse the two.

Young men and women participate in conditioning and the excitement and harshness of missions enabling them to live out a version of themselves based on the promises and pressures of their military peers and supervisors. While we have indications of the types of people drawn to these environments, it has not been explored fully. During my years treating military veterans, I must say that I have never seen information about their enrollment interviews—their personal issues, concerns, personalities, possible histories of abuse or neglect, or their families of origin. Why not? I guess we could argue that recruiters and medical personnel on the front end don't have the training or the time. We could also argue that recruiting pressures means that quotas must be met, so a lot of complicated questions are simply not asked about recruit traits that might signal a high likelihood of problems down the road.

When it comes to OSIs, based on recent research and observations, it can be argued that much of the brain's rewiring, often attributed to combat reactions, likely occurred during military conditioning. Specifically, repeated messages about specialness hinging on things like emotional suppression, compartmentalization, and functional dissociation (detached persona) may have already done their jobs. I also believe that clinicians encounter narcissistic injuries all the time across a broad range of clientele whether they realize it or not. When it comes to military clientele, the good news is that their basic anxieties about vulnerability continue to represent their connection to humanness—and hence their hope of recovery. The real task for them and for helpers is to value this vulnerability and possible injuries to selfhood without emasculating them and risking further shame. I also believe that the emerging interventions like mindfulness, yoga, acceptance and commitment therapy, and emotion-focused therapies may allow for the safe relaxation of self-restraint (decompression) and offer the possibility of real change. While proponents of these approaches have unproven theories about what they are actually doing, they seem to have the advantage of not focusing exclusively on decontextualized management of symptoms and thoughts.

Eleven

Making Aggressive Brains

As a young man, I wore our flag on my shoulder with pride, and after leaving the military I stitched it on backpacks while traveling through Western Europe. My experience, however, is fundamentally different than that of other soldiers. A veteran who had been active in Somalia said to me, "I hated the military for giving me all that pride, and I hated myself for believing in it. It was all a fucking lie, and I don't know if I'll ever believe in anything ever again."

⌒

As Hoge articulated succinctly, Western militaries over generations have perfected the psychological processes of transforming youngsters into soldiers capable of killing. The introduction to overbearing drill sergeants and NCOs and exposing recruits to demanding and unfamiliar commands starts this transformation process of disorientation and strain. The initial weeks without contact with the outside are carefully orchestrated and based on previous experiences with hundreds of thousands of recruits. These strategies aim specifically at loosening ties with the civilian world and weakening one's former sense of identity. Training presents an ever-increasing set of demands to meet—each designed to create apprehension and a personal challenge to be overcome. Make no mistake: this is designed as a psychological process along with the well-advertised references to skills acquisition. Through tactics that do not usually contravene the Geneva Convention or the Canadian Charter of Human Rights, it is meant to be a respectful albeit dehumanizing experience nonetheless. To be clear, my use of the word *dehumanizing* should not be confused with words like the *degradation, humiliation,* or *torture.* Instead, I am referring to the processes required to produce automatic, unconscious behaviors that require trainees to suppress emotional vulnerability and steel themselves psychologically. Having said this, our special forces personnel have an entirely different perspective on the role of things like torture that may be required for training purposes. Recruits must be taught how to overcome fear and to master aggression by developing a detached persona that hinges on disconnection from their inner experiences and submission to commands and to the group. In fact, I think that there may be a type of dissociation at work that facilitates the development of this emotionally detached version of the self. The result of all this is an earned sense of pride in oneself and indeed in the larger organization.

Soldier pride also revolves around a newly acquired or amplified ability to act automatically and aggressively as directed. The ability to harness energy and perform under pressure when commanded is an infinitely valuable personal asset within the military. It allows soldiers to be reshaped as lethal weapons. From a psychological standpoint, military conditioning represents a process of repeatedly exposing members to fear and even terror in situations from which there is no escape (i.e., habituation and desensitization). Aggression becomes the solution to overcome helplessness. Soldiers learn how to harness this energy and to submit to the group in order to do things they would not otherwise even consider. It represents nothing less than an altered state of being for many young men and women.

The ability to transform any emotional energy into aggression is valuable for soldiers' self-management. It allows them to harness mind-numbing and muscle-freezing adrenaline surges and to use this energy for automatic action upon command while avoiding preemptive actions or freezing. It is a delicately balanced and essential skill. It is supported by repeated mental rehearsal of things like tactics and arcs (specified degree angles for the field of fire for a projectile weapon), ROEs, situational awareness, and strategies like tactical breathing (a technique used by soldiers to control physical overarousal). In a real sense, their brains and nervous systems are retuned to tightly controlled, hair-trigger reactivity. I believe that this mental conditioning in situational control and self-restraint offers a partial explanation of the oft-noted denial of vulnerability among soldiers in any sphere of their lives—they are always at some level of prepared alertness. And they have learned that prepared alertness works because it got them through demanding training and kept them and others safe in dangerous places. Many of them tell me that they have lost their off switch—they cannot find acceptable ways to relax or to discharge emotional tension in order to reset. This is the price to be paid for military conditioning.

We need to understand that the soldier is a weapon of war and not a particular new toy that goes bang. These men and women are the product of intensive training and tactics that recreates them as lethal combatants controlled by lawful commands and fully prepared and capable of killing. This weapon must be controlled in a solid container—bound by ethics, values, discipline, and acting only under specific orders—so that this weapon does not go off unintentionally. But sometimes it does escape in war zones—soldiers overcome with grief or rage can go "off the reservation." Over the years, veterans have told me about instances in places like Somalia, Bosnia, and Afghanistan where things "just needed to be done." It can also go off in the form of aggression and physical fights, bullying, and even attempts to harm specific leaders. This is not meant to fuel the outlandish Hollywood characterization of the dangerous veteran. In my experience, this depiction is completely inaccurate in the Canadian context. In fact, soldiers and veterans are more likely to self-manage by going in the opposite direction through overcontrol, social avoidance, and shutting down. While they may contend with persistent aggressive thoughts and impulses, their conditioning in self-restraint and acting only under command usually serves as an incredibly powerful damper.

Cognitive dissonance theory explains some of the disorientation experienced by veterans. Because of their investments and the rewards from an established military persona, they often interpret their difficulties after service as inadequacies in their families and communities. Someone must be wrong, and it is psychologically easier to blame civilian society rather than question their engrained military value system or their overinflated sense of themselves. Similarly, dissonance also explains how experienced harms or mistreatment of colleagues cannot be acknowledged. Two opposite realities cannot be true simultaneously in a rigid, black-and-white world. When members turn their backs on distressed buddies or keep instances of abuse to themselves, then the central values of loyalty and brotherhood begin to unravel. A less distressing mental position for members who live by the military family mantra is to view instances of mistreatment of themselves and others as aberrations or the fault of personal weakness. Soldiers attempt to protect themselves psychologically by believing one over the other to reduce emotional turmoil. In the interest of continuing to invest in their roles, unfortunately, it is less distressing to blame those who are affected. This is aided by other mental strategies, including outright denial, rationalization, minimization, or intellectualization.

In the 1960s, Leon Festinger[lvi] argued that extended exposure to mental conflicts can create emotional reactions that are managed by these types of psychological processes. If these strategies do not resolve the conflict or if emotional reactions cannot be managed, then other reactions can develop into problems including bouts of unexplained anger, anxiety, depression, or traumatic stress reactions. For example, the military is promoted as a brotherhood, but for the soldier who believes that he was thrown away when he was injured, either the brotherhood ideal is a lie or he must have been a "shit-pump." When veterans default to the latter explanation to resolve the turmoil linked with medical discharges, the groundwork is laid for chronic difficulties in moving forward in civilian life.

When people leave the military, no matter the circumstance, they might all benefit from a predetermined period of psychological reconditioning. This does not mean they must learn to throw away everything they learned in the military. On the contrary, we should acknowledge that some of these qualities are necessary and important in general society. It does mean candidly reminding them that the persona they were taught had the specific purpose of meeting the needs of the military, nothing more or less. Otherwise, when veterans are not prepared for the letdown and internal conflicts following their release dates, the ensuing sense of loss and unexplained emptiness can

be very distressing. These can contribute to unexplained physical complaints and mental distress. In the absence of awareness of these normal reactions—which can last several years or
longer—people can be left quite defenseless.

In my work, I have met many veterans who had been out of the
military for varying periods of time. Many of them would certainly meet the official criteria for an OSI, but others did not report
key events. It seems obvious that the psychological consequences
of leaving the military can develop into bona fide mental-health
problems over time. Soldiers are not aware of the significance of
the uniform to their central identity or of how much former ranks
and military occupations defined their relationships and indeed
who they were as people in the world.

Twelve

Believers and Chameleons

*I don't want to be one of the bitter and twisted ones like
a lot of the guys I used to know in the navy. When we
made all the changes and lost true camaraderie, a lot
of them just reached their piss-off points and walked
away. My final straw came when I saw discrimination
happening on my last ship. I tried to push it up to
the admiral's desk and was simply told that even as
the chief it was not my place to challenge policy, so
I just waited and made the leap to another job.*

Dave spent thirty-two years in the navy on numerous deployments
and managed to transfer to a civil service position. He told me that
he drinks too much, can't sleep, has no hobbies or interests, and
spends most of his days at work simply occupying time: "I just sit and
shake my head and say whatever and do what they ask me. You know
you have been around too long when we are arguing about the same
problems we had in the eighties. It never changes—same shit, different day." I asked him why he did not leave or transfer to another

department. When Dave started to tell me that it was only about the money, I pushed the point with him for an honest answer. He said, "I joined at eighteen from northern Manitoba. The military is all I have ever known, and I don't know if I could survive in another job. I know I can't keep doing this; it's killing me, but I don't think I have anywhere else to go. All my buddies are gone now. It's just me and my wife, and she does not even talk to me anymore."

All first-response organizations target young, impressionable, and even vulnerable youngsters and put them through various forms of skills training couched in idealism. When it is over and members are worn out or they see through the arbitrariness and emptiness of specialness, systems have little choice but to spit them out and leave them to reconcile themselves, essentially on their own. Unfortunately, this is also true of our national and local police forces, paramedics, and firefighters. There is simply no room in the day-to-day organization of work roles in these institutions for those who cannot play along. And we certainly cannot publicly acknowledge possible downsides of this conditioning and training— it is all presumed to be positive in turning young men and women into responsible and contributing citizens. One consequence of our inability to acknowledge the possible downsides of militaristic conditioning is that we end up with ill-informed and halfhearted efforts that fail to address the ongoing problem of dislocation among veterans. The problems of broken families, unemployment, addiction, and suicides seem to top the list of consequences. Instead, we attempt to explain veteran dislocation by focusing on things like financial pressures, personal stressors, or the legacies of their families of origin.

As I have said previously, equating the felt sensations of aggression in one's body—alertness and readiness to act—with being fully alive can lead one to feel like the walking dead in its absence. A veteran of Afghanistan told me, "Nothing can replace that, so now I have no reason to even get out of bed anymore." Military and paramilitary organizations do not seem capable of comprehending the fact that when they introduce soldiers to their capacity for lethal aggression, it does not dissipate simply because they no longer wear a uniform. It persists even when these people want to forget their mental conditioning—it is automatic, which was the point of training in the first place. They are expected to rein in and manage this on their own: "They gave me this ability [to kill and destroy] and then they took the switch from me." Veterans describe being without orders anymore and not having ways of knowing when to use or not use this ability. Again, this is not meant to support existing veteran stereotypes. I just mean that soldiers are often left to manage themselves, usually through stoic silence and overcontrol.

In a real sense, the Canadian soldier is a national emblem periodically needed as a distraction from other immediate social problems, like poverty, addiction, and suicide facing our First Nations peoples, the ongoing opioid crisis, child poverty and abuse, and domestic violence. Instead, we occupy ourselves with the near mythical battles of places like Vimy Ridge and conveniently forget that many of these World War I veterans were neglected; some were left to destitution upon their return to Canada. We seem unable to weave the hard lessons from places like Passchendaele, Ypres, Dieppe, or Beaumont Hamel into a balanced national narrative. We also exclude from the story those young Canadians who were executed for desertion during these campaigns;[lvii] many were later deemed to be suffering from shell shock. Instead, revered war images of other remembered battles, whether true or fantastical, are dredged up from history to serve purposes that have very little to do with the motivations or the conduct of modern warfare. They are meant to promote a carefully crafted image of the Canadian soldier.

These stirring images also serve the purpose of indoctrinating our children and reminding the public of strange phrases about uncommon valor, bravery, pride, and protecting Canada. Yet veterans from both the Great Wars had little choice but to engage in protests, sometimes deadly, over a response of neglect to their mental and physical injuries—governments who decided that they simply did not have the money to spend on veterans. So, men like my great-uncle Paul from World War I and my uncle George from World War II returned home to nothing following these wars. To be fair, history tells us that many of our World War II veterans fared much better than their World War I counterparts; Canada had seemed to learn the hard lessons from its mismanagement of veterans returning from World War I.

Men and women returning from wars as mental casualties stand in opposition to our cherished clichés and show us the price that is paid to help manage our ongoing confusion over national identity. They also present us with the costs of wars— no matter how noble or exciting the cause for the participants or those at home. These men and women present us with global realities—hatred, brutality, greed, and unacknowledged economic and trade interests wrapped up in our own near-religious ideals. In a peculiar twist, there are few places for men and women who have been tarnished by engaging in these realities; they are no longer welcome among the rest of us. I don't think we can blame average people for their reactions. How could it be otherwise?

On the heels of the war in Afghanistan, a new buzz phrase has emerged—*military to civilian transition* (MCT). It is meant to describe the difficulties facing many former military people. This bureaucratic term is usually confined to pragmatic and important considerations about such things as the need for financial supports, employment and education opportunities, and improved medical care. But this notion of transition is based on a shallow sentimentality. In fact, there is no such thing as transition for many military veterans. They describe reentering the civil world as requiring a complete metamorphosis from who they were in uniform. This redefinition of self asks that they give up the uniqueness of being a soldier and undergo mental reconditioning.

Our accepted notion of transition seems to miss a central problem among many veterans—the drive to recreate specialness. The term, by definition, denotes a smooth, almost effortless move from one thing to another. It is a useful metaphor for politicians and bureaucrats alike. But it belies much harsher realities for many veterans for whom leaving the military is often experienced as jarring, abrupt, and disorienting. Even when veterans leave of their own accord, the idea of transitioning does not apply since they have no ideas about what to expect with the loss of their former status. For those who are medically released, most of them describe a difficult transition. This seems to be directly influenced by several things: (a) having no control over the decision, (b) lingering physical or mental-health problems, and (c) having no realistic opportunity to recreate specialness.

My wife reminds me that at one level, the experience of joining the military is similar in some respects to joining medical professions. Transitioning into the system comes with attention to skills developments, mentoring, assistance, guidance, and scrutiny to ensure competencies as trainees taking on their respective professional identities. When it comes to the military, however, Carl

Castro noted that the first two years form a critical point in terms of suicide risk. In 2016, a Canadian admiral was quoted as saying that it usually takes up to five years before sailors are fully indoctrinated into the military system. I think we should ask, then, about the things that happen at the back end—when people leave. Certainly, the process does not resemble the initial phases.

In the normal course, releases occur relatively quickly; in cases of medical release, the timeframes can be protracted, allowing time for the bureaucracy to process them out. However, things like mentoring, specific retraining for civilian life, or skills assessments of one's ability to meet the demands of civilian life are not entertained. Even in the civilian world, many retirees face anonymity and lack of relevance and are heading back to the workforce. Many commentators believe that this is financially driven, but this is not true for many of them. They also miss specialness and the sense of purpose in an otherwise boring world. They also want to recreate feelings of competence and importance and to reconnect tangibly with their former identity.[lviii]

The experience of leaving the military can present a mix of emotions: initial relief is quickly followed by boredom and the recognition of loss. Time can become a prison. It may sound somewhat ironic, but newly found freedom can also produce panic. The constriction and containment provided through military roles, codes of conduct, rules, and structure also provided psychological stability and assurance. When this is removed, the reaction can be one of loss of mental bearings. Psychologist and author Joseph Burgo[lix] coined the phrase *terror of disintegration*; it may be a fitting term to describe intense anxiety and panic reactions among some veterans contending with the loss of former identity. As a CAF Army veteran said to me, "You know nothing bad happened to me in the military. Since I left, I am anxious all the time. I just have to be around uniforms to feel safe."

A different example may help demonstrate this point. When our son arrived home from the hospital, my wife would wrap him tightly in a blanket—swaddling—and even though he would struggle against the confines of the blanket it was also the only way he would settle enough to sleep. The constricting containment simultaneously provided assurances of safety. I think about this in the context of those leaving the military—it is like being thrown to the world. The strict structural boundaries offered from the internalization of ideals and values and submission to the group, while confining, also provided a basis for mental stability. Outside in the civilian world, this container is replaced with broad and nebulous rules and absence of feedback on proper conduct.

Military people can't possibly realize how important this structure truly is until they lose it. When I discuss this continued search for specialness among veterans, some appear uncomfortable and even embarrassed initially. For many others, it provides a forum for them to finally acknowledge a central struggle. Among those veterans who continue to search out important causes after leaving the military, I often wonder whether these efforts offer them peace of mind. It seems to me that they are attempting to fill a bottomless pit. As soon as the newest venture is over and they are once again forgotten, I often see them slip into depression and withdrawal. Their fundamental questions about self-worth have not been answered. I think it is important that they eventually face themselves if they are ever to come to terms with damaged pride and self-worth. Admittedly, this is a tricky topic since we are still in the very early days of attempting to understand the effects of conditioning and specialness on the mental health of military members and other first responders. We must steadfastly resist any efforts to simply blame operational-stress injuries on the broken ones, however.

In fact, when we speak of transitions to civilian life, there are multiple postmilitary life trajectories that are quite varied depending on factors like age of retirement, intergenerational family connections to the military, service element(s), length of time in the military, or whether they were regular or reserve force. The biggest determinant of postservice success seems to be whether soldiers left of their own accord in relatively good health or whether they were medically discharged. This mix of variables produces wide discrepancies for their expected life trajectories. I believe the MCT problem requires attention beyond pragmatic issues—many veterans are left on their own to confront the strangeness of who they have become as people and the experience of being dumped back into a world that is often foreign to them. By all accounts, these effects are much more pronounced for younger veterans in the prime of life who seem devoid of purpose. According to American research and emerging Canadian research, the two-year period postservice seems to be an acutely stressful and risky time for many of these men and women.[lx]

The process of veteran transition can in some respects be captured by the notion of *reverse culture shock*. This term has been coined to describe the disorientation and dislocation suffered by some people when they return home after years overseas. It can result in unexpected difficulties in readjusting to one's home culture and the values of their home country. An Afghanistan veteran said to me, "When I got home from tour, I didn't go out in public because these fucking people just made me sick to my stomach, fat and lazy with their whining little brats…All of them focused on what they can get." The previously familiar has become unfamiliar and intolerable. We know that soldiers of all eras who deployed overseas describe a need to readjust upon return, and the military leadership has taken it seriously. New regulations provide for extended periods of leave following over-seas deployments, and recent changes remove personnel from the deployment cycle for a year or more.

Even so, I don't think that reverse culture shock explana-tions or attention to extended readjustment periods adequately capture the combined legacy of military ideology, societal con-tradictions, and the direct experiences of many people leaving the military. In contrast, their psychological connection to mili-tarism and especially the denial of vulnerability seems to con-tribute to lasting cultural disconnects. After all, these men and women have participated in a mental-emotional world that is strikingly different and separated from the civilian world they left behind. When it comes to mental distress, again specialness creates additional twists for military veterans in terms of who they believe can understand their unique struggles and who can be trusted enough to offer them help.

If they grew up in a highly structured military family and even if they came from chaotic backgrounds and joined the military as teenagers, in fact, they are not transitioning back to the civil-ian world. They are psychologically and emotionally entering civil-ian culture for the first time. A navy veteran said to me, "My old man was army, so I spent my life on military bases. I was fourteen years old before I even heard the word *civilian*. I joined the cadets and the navy when I was old enough…Been out for almost fifteen years, and I still don't get it. I still don't fit. I am an older guy now, but I still think about rejoining almost every day."

For many veterans, retirement can be an exciting time filled with the promise of new opportunities, but for others their de-partures are filled with all the insecurities and lack of confi-dence that leaving home entails for most of us. There is one unmistakable difference, however. Many of these veterans are now much older and hardened mentally and emotionally. They often struggle with a profound sense of disorientation and dislocation that does not necessarily improve with the simple passage of time. Many of them spiral into problems with addiction, isolation, loss of marriages, incarceration, and multiple failed attempts at stable work. Some eventually end up filling the ranks of the homeless, or they end their lives. So, the notion of transition as we understand it seems quite inadequate.

There are many veterans who never get past the longing to go back and to belong once again. They display a nostalgic yearning for reconnection, predictability, and specialness. It can be heart wrenching to watch them struggle year after year with the loss of the essence of who they were as confident and proud men and women. I don't think we should sanitize this reality by overreliance on abstract, clinical language about mental illness. We should not overdramatize the seriousness of their struggles either. But until we have real conversations and make real efforts to acknowledge the depth of their experiences of loss and dislocation, our efforts will likely continue to be lacking.

Despite the well-meaning efforts of the military hierarchy, we can't really expect them to accomplish this work because they simply can't truly understand it until they have the experience of being a former military member just like the rest of us. And when they do leave, their observations and insights can be discounted because they become like the rest of us—yesterday's forgotten heroes.

We draw on many references to the men and women of World War II as the real Canadian soldier, but there are many differences between these people and modern-day veterans. In his book *Those Who Have Borne the Battle,*[lxi] James Wright lays out the case of an increasingly unrepresentative military in the United States. In

Canada, a former CAF surgeon general, Hans Jung, came to a similar appraisal, stating that our military is overrepresented by young white males with family ties to the military: "The recruitment pool for the CF has traditionally been fit young men between the ages of seventeen and twenty-four, coming from rural areas or from urban areas with a population of less than one hundred thousand. Recruits have generally been white males with previous familial CF ties, possessing a high-school education or less."[lxii]

Many of them join as youngsters and stay with the promise of a lifelong career. If we take Jung's analysis at face value, I believe it raises the notion of military family dynasties and its implications for military to civilian maladjustment. It is also an off-handed acknowledgment of the importance of one's military pedigree—formally and informally—within the promotion system. Good pedigrees increase the chances for early-career mentoring and fast-tracking through the ranks. In the face of continual societal changes, an unbroken lineage ensures the protection of central values, customs, and traditions of the military ethos. I believe that this is the true fabric of the institution, one that has been handed down from fathers to sons over generations. The downside is that it offers a partial explanation for the seeming intractability of the military and like-minded institutions from enacting fundamental cultural change.

As noted by the Vanier Institute and emerging research into military families in Canada, while there are certainly positive experiences for military families, they also face significant mental-emotional challenges. Like their parents, children of military parents learn to be pragmatic, self-reliant, and grow accustomed to being uprooted—the only constant is the military institution and other military families. Basic attachment styles, interpersonal and communication patterns, masculine and conservative ideologies often reflect those they learned from being around the larger military. In a sense, military children are the living legacy of the military institution—many join the cadet movement, militias, and eventually join the military or other first-response organizations.

In fact, among the RCMP veterans I have seen, many of them also grew up in military or policing families. Of course, there are those children who will rebel and wish to have nothing to do with the military. Understandably, many of them eventually end up in other first-response organizations. The point is that when these people leave the military, they are losing on two fronts—they are losing the continuity of extended family traditions and connection to the military as well as their own military buddies and units. The adjustment for these people would be similar in some ways to landing on a new planet in terms of disorientation and dislocation. I think special efforts should be directed toward these men and women.

When they leave, many veterans will face all those personal insecurities and perceived weaknesses they spent a lifetime learning to hide or overcome. These challenges often must be resolved as they begin to decompress and make the shift into community life. This time, however, they do not have the benefit of routine military structure and expected roles or rank—relevance and authority—to help them. Requirements like relinquishing the need for constant mental preparedness, risking vulnerability, acknowledging secret desires to depend on others, or discovering playfulness or innocence become important things to address. These qualities are vital for genuine social reconnection, but unfortunately these things are often denigrated as "touchy-feely" nonsense by pragmatic people.

The good news is that many veterans do take the risk to relinquish some of what they learned from the military to make room for a more hopeful and connected existence. Some veterans allude to these changes with statements like this: "Man, if my old RSM or my buddies could see me now, I am not sure what they would think about me." A difficult challenge to overcome is the preoccupation with reputation and control that prevents soldiers from admitting to vulnerability or needing others close to them to understand and accept them. It is the never-ending struggle against the "shared separateness" they grew accustomed to during life in uniform. While soldiers can be loyal to one another as needed or respond to orders, every member is essentially preoccupied with his self-image apart from other people. And this separateness, even if it is aimed at being the special one or the go-to guy in the unit, can be the breeding ground for profound loneliness and disconnection.

Admission of loneliness and the desire to be emotionally close to others are taboo topics in the military and many other first-response organizations. Reliance on others and interdependence is simply not an acceptable quality—not yet at least. Desires for intimacy or connection continue to be reflected somewhat immaturely in sexualized language and through linkages with the feminine; these needs and desires cannot be acknowledged even after retirement. But change may be on the way. Despite all the hand wringing about the problem of the millennials, I think that these young men and women may finally help us come to terms with the outdated value system of rugged individuality. They are also a generation that is challenging accepted norms around stoicism, sexuality, and keeping their emotions to themselves; they want to think for themselves. They seem less attracted to traditional workplaces, including our established institutions. This shift seems to coincide with a social crisis among the previous generation—the continuing displacement of traditional masculine roles and suicides among white, North American males.[lxiii] From the men I see, there is often a wistful yearning for assured male values and roles of the past that seem to be related to the changing nature of workplace expectations and our evolving understanding of modern men and women.

A fundamental question I often hear from military veterans is "Who am I as a person?" Some people choose not to explore the answer because of the fear of uncertainty or because they cannot find the courage to face what they may have lost of themselves over the years. These existential questions do not fit neatly in mental illness diagnoses or respond very well to our standard interventions. Of course, the conversation that seldom occurs among veterans is the one acknowledging the sacrifices made by spouses and children in the name of their careers.

Thirteen

Always Needing More

"What in the name of the good goddamned Jesus H. Christ are you doing with that weapon, Maggot?" Jake caught sight of the master corporal making a beeline in his direction. "Listen here, boy, when I give the command to present arms, that is what you will do…I don't want to see that weapon waving around like a goddamned umbrella! Do you understand me?"

Jake replied, "Yes, Master Corporal."

Moving to within inches of Jake's face, the instructor screamed even louder: "I can't hear you!"

He responded with an equally loud answer with all the contained venom he could muster: "Yes, Master Corporal!"

Jake woke up, covered in sweat, and immediately pissed off. Five hours later two police cruisers roar into his driveway for the second time since last Saturday. This time it was his wife who called for help. Last time it was a neighbor who Jake had threatened for shoveling snow onto his driveway. He was ready for them. "Do you know who I am? Do you realize what I can do to you? I can put you and these other guys down before you even realize what is happening here."

This had been Jake's way of dealing with people since leaving the military a year ago. He secretly enjoyed the shocked look on their faces; it gave him control again. He wanted respect; all the power he had as the chief warrant officer had evaporated, and he risked being just another nobody. In the military, rank and authority had given him all he needed to deal with any challenger, including the officers—nobody messed with him. His secret mantra was to never let anybody know they were getting to him, never let anybody know when insults or the racial stuff hurt. He learned to hide it from view, to hold onto it and wait for the right time to get them back. But here he was consumed by a seventeen-year-old son who would not listen to anything he said and who was intent on challenging Jake in physical fights, saying things like, "We did fine without you here. You don't get to come back in our house and try to tell me what to do. Your days to be daddy are long gone, old man."

Jake told me about his introduction to the military and about a corporal who refused to allow him in the junior ranks mess as a private because of his skin color. He harbored his hatred for this man until years later when the opportunity came for payback when they were both sergeants. A disagreement between their subordinates required that the two senior NCOs intervene. It was a Friday evening. Jake had been unwinding over a few drinks when the phone rang. He agreed to meet the other man in the office downstairs to discuss the problem. The sergeant opened the office door to be met by a roundhouse punch that knocked him unconscious. Jake simply closed the door and walked back up the stairs to his room and resumed drinking—this was the power of hatred. This was how he resolved problems in the past, and he was not about to change for anybody.

Jake kept his private issues to himself. Growing up poor in a small community surrounded by white people who always reminded him of his second-rate status. He was the first in his family to join the military; it was his way out. He found the same things in the military; they weren't widespread but were in small pockets here and there. Nobody knew about the devastation he felt from the death of his first child when he was away on deployment decades earlier or his sense of failure as a father to guide his son who was repeatedly in trouble with the law. Jake's solution had been to ignore these things and drive his efforts into his career, which meant volunteering for anything thrown his way. It had worked— he had been accepted into special units, participated in clandestine missions, and traveled quickly through the ranks.

But it had not been enough. He was always in debt financially because of retail therapy and the never-ending need for new toys—new trucks, new cars; it was always a new something, no matter the cost. It was the only way he had known to forget the embarrassment he had felt for his own father—a Jamaican immigrant who put up with degrading comments and mistreatment in their small community to keep his job to support the family. That was not going to be Jake.

Six months after retirement, Jake had his first trip to a hospital emergency room and was diagnosed with severe panic by the emergency room physician. He reluctantly took the doctor's advice to talk with someone about his mental health. The counselor immediately presented Jake with the possibility of operational PTSD as the cause of his problems. Well, maybe, thought Jake. He had certainly seen enough stuff in various places in the Middle East, including Afghanistan, but was that the reason he felt so messed up out here with his wife and his son? Was that the reason he did not seem to have a place among them? Sure, because of his roles he knew many secrets about the military that would never be discussed and other things about the military he would never say publicly. His reputation among his peers mattered too much, and even on the outside he needed to protect his legacy—his image as the chief. He would uphold his end of his agreement to the CAF and to his former colleagues at all costs.

When it comes to the image and reputation of the CAF, soldiers learn to be political minded. They will defend their reputations—national clichés—as members of the institution or risk the label of interloper. This means keeping their private realities separate from their public persona. The star colonel, the epitome of professionalism, may terrorize his wife in drunken rages at home or the police sergeant may spend his off-hours fantasizing about sexual encounters to feel something. As said to me many times over the years, "The military is a game of perceptions and performance." Soldiers are taught that civilians can never understand, that the media can't be trusted, and above all that they are never to bring discredit to the uniform. They are caught up in the near fanatical preoccupation with image within our public institutions. These narratives are carefully crafted, as evidenced by the incremental growth of public affairs departments in many of our public institutions.

In stark contrast to their military ethos, to benefit from talk therapies, personnel must be willing to relinquish control. This can be a monumental task for those who have spent their lives under rigid self-restraint. Accepting help means trusting strangers with their welfare, talking about themselves, and digging into closely guarded secrets about themselves. All the while, they have to contend with their paramount concerns over self-image. Remember, nearly everything about military life comes down to image. Many simply cannot accept this level of risk. They play along or end these relationships prematurely because it is too disorienting; soldiers are always to be in control.

My clinical and research work has taught me that those people who grew up in challenging environments—estimated to be around one-third of all children in Canada—[lxiv] are the ones more likely to overinvest in military ethos. They seem to have the toughest time admitting to vulnerability of any type. Those who experienced fragmented families or abuse—and there are a substantial number of them—often view the military as the only family they have ever known. I believe that they may be more susceptible to the effects of conditioning on their fundamental identity compared to those members who remain grounded psychologically within their biological families and communities. This dichotomy contributes to their continual internal struggles over specialness versus worthlessness.

I don't believe that we can discuss this yearning for specialness without also mentioning notions of narcissism and self-absorption. In my mind, they serve as primary strategies to enable people to overcome basic self-worth questions. Of course, the opposite of these qualities are things like humility and even gratitude for the wondrous gift of life in this world—an attitude that acknowledges that our presence here is purely accidental and will be experienced for a finite time. Nobody is getting out alive. This alternative attitude can make all the difference, I believe. With this attitude, people can realize that the only thing "more" to be obtained is moments of connection to something, preferably genuine connection to other people. Military people are used to intense involvement in situations and with other people centering on risk and danger.

Often, they get to witness and participate in extraordinary things that show the best of human nature even in the face of the worst of human nature. Danger and risk occupy, by default, the full attention even of civilians; our physical beings become alert to every breath, every nuance of movement, and every thought. This way of feeling alive seems to be the thing that is missing for many veterans—this singular focus in the moment. For many of them, chasing the adrenaline train is a difficult habit to break.

Fourteen

Ten Feet Tall and Bulletproof

"Jeez, Mark, I think that's an ax in Sammy's hand!" Gill alerted his partner to the large man, apparently drunk, staggering from his doorstep headed in their direction. They knew Sammy; they had been called many times to come to his house, usually after the government checks had been issued to the First Nations reserve.

Gill tried again to get his attention. "Hey, Sammy whatsya' doin' man? It's me, Gill. Why don't you put that thing down so we can talk?"

Sammy was not in any mood to talk. Inside the house, his wife was bleeding badly from punches to her face. Sammy had turned on her again today. He knew that one look from the RCMP officers meant he would be going to jail. His speech was thick from the effects of the alcohol. "As soon as you talk to my woman, I know what's gonna happen. I'm not in any mood to go to your cells today."

Sammy picked up his pace, swinging the ax wildly in Gill's direction. There was no choice left now but to draw his weapon. He yelled to Sammy to drop the ax. No response! A second later, Gill's round slammed into Sammy at midchest, knocking him backward. The two officers approached the downed man and kicked the ax away before trying to determine his injuries. Sammy was seriously injured, but he'd live. Gill thought to himself, Yup, and we'll probably be doing this all over again in a month or so; it's like a never-ending *Groundhog Day* like that Bill Murray movie. His service revolver seemed to spend more time out of his holster than in it. What a difference from other officers who talked about spending their careers never having to draw their weapons. Just another day in the Wild West.

While recounting this story, Gill looked at me and smiled: "It's almost funny. That was an average day in Northern Alberta… Murders, suicides…stupid, drunken accidental deaths on all-terrain vehicles, fires, you name it. On Friday and Saturday nights, we would not even respond to calls; we would simply lock the detachment doors and turn off the lights. It would be mayhem out there. You just couldn't risk going out."

Gill told me a lot more about his time in the North. "You really wonder if you're having any effect at all or if you were just transported to hell as some kind of a joke. I got to a point where I just did not give a shit anymore. I mean, I was taking a lot of stupid risks where I could easily have been killed, but I just didn't care. Really. I look back on that now, and it all just seems like a bad dream."

Gill grew up in a navy family. His dad was gone a lot, leaving his mother to rule the house like a sergeant major even when his father was home. "I think we had it good overall. I mean, we didn't move around very much, which was good. Dad was a bit of a drinker when he would get home but nothing crazy; he always did stuff with us. I think it was pretty normal. Don't get me wrong: we definitely knew right from wrong, we knew the importance of standing up for our values and not taking shit from other people. I think these were all good lessons."

In terms of the costs of his twenty-year career in the RCMP, Gill tells me that he learned quickly in the system that he was essentially on his own. His main supporter, his wife, had decided she had had enough about ten years before and had filed for divorce. Gill said:

She just couldn't adjust to those shit holes and always wondering if I'd be making it back home in one piece...Guess I can't blame her. We're friends today, which is good. Ya know, nobody is looking out for you, not like the military. They did nothing for me, even when I told them I was having some issues; my line officer just looked at me and didn't say one word to me. Nothing. So, I just felt like I was standing with my back to the edge of a cliff, always trying to keep my balance by continually pushing or risk ending up over the edge. I kept doing my job kicking down doors for another six months before pulling myself out—I was just too reckless, a danger to my guys.

From the day I went off ODS [off-duty sick], it was like I was contagious. Nobody called. Not even my guys. It's like they did not know what to say to me anymore. I would see a few of them around and ask what the problem was. I tried to tell them that I was still me, but it was always awkward. So, I got this call to come in and clear out my locker. I got there and found the lock already cut off. My stuff was crammed into a box in the corner of an office. I lost my shit; that really pissed me off, so I made a complaint directly to the superintendent. Screw them. I decided that I was going to stand up for myself because nobody else would, and I was not going to hang my head. I've got nothing to apologize for. The RCMP needs to get its head out of its own ass.

～

Gill's story is like that of many others I have seen for OSIs of all types and from all eras. There is something fundamentally similar for all of us in uniform. I think it centers on pride in oneself and the job. It comes from being acknowledged for being good, maybe even the best, at something. Also, the drive toward commitment to the job and being recognized as special can be simply too enticing to ignore. These are the all-in ones, the go-to people, and the ones others look up to; they are the ones invested in specialness. To be that person means jettisoning anything that gets in the way: families must be sacrificed, hobbies and interests must be put on a back burner, the inconsistencies and arbitrariness of the system must be blocked out, imagination and spontaneity must be extinguished, potential weaknesses must be hidden, and the civilian world must be pushed completely out of consciousness. When veterans speak about feeling betrayed and abandoned, I believe they are also referring to these unacknowledged but expected sacrifices that they made for their uniformed brethren. The reality is that our institutions depend on these people to function, but usually they cannot be acknowledged. A navy veteran told me, "The ship can't sail without you…just one more trip and then you can go ashore and see the medical people."

Here's the thing: Our military institution has incorporated an identity of silent professionalism in response to chronic underfunding and underappreciation over recent generations. Members are proud of the fact of punching above their weight and making do with the available resources. The expectation to step up and fill operational gaps is shared, which means that individual members cannot be acknowledged without alerting senior leadership to resource problems. Everyone is expected to make do with less. I think this internal reality is a breeding ground for resentment of civil society and our political leaders.

The veterans whom we have treated were commonly adopted as children; had absent, demanding, or abusive parents; came from divorced families; or had one or both parents with serious mental-health or addiction problems. And what has this got to do with military PTSD resolution? Understandably, these men and women often have considerable problems relying on other people because of early-life relational ruptures. They learned that adults could not be trusted to look out for them—and then they received institutional messages about dependability and self-reliance. Their presentation of being highly independent, self-contained, and resilient people often makes them star performers in organizations like the military, police, firefighting, and paramedicine.

I wonder whether lingering military trauma reactions are expressed in too much self-restraint and constricted emotional reactivity. The personal things that cannot ever be shared with another person or even put into words can still cause us problems. Internal experiences and reactions to external events that cannot be made visible because there is no vehicle can still wreak havoc in our lives. In my experience, once these experiences can become something and be validated—an image drawn on paper, an honest conversation with a buddy, a fleeting facial expression that is noticed—they can start the process of resolution. A something that is tangible, touchable, or observable can become solvable. Soldiers and first responders do need ways to unpack their invisible rucksacks.

David Grossman is a former American soldier and psychologist who wrote about the psychological costs of killing. He reminds us of the powerful, innate human resistance toward killing one's own species and the psychological mechanisms developed by armies over centuries to overcome that resistance. These techniques have been applied with tremendous success in modern combat training to condition soldiers to overcome this natural resistance to killing. For Grossman, killing is a private, intimate experience of tremendous intensity, in which the destructive act becomes psychologically very much like the procreative act. Attempting to understand this through the cultural mythology of Hollywood is about as useful as trying to feel the intimacy of a sexual relationship by watching pornographic movies.

With the proper conditioning and the proper circumstances, it appears that almost anyone can and will kill. But the secret truth that flies in the face of the warrior mythology is that throughout history the majority of men on the battlefield would not attempt to kill the enemy, even to save their own lives or the lives of their friends. The weak link between the killing potential and the killing capability of these units was the soldier. The simple fact is that when faced with a living, breathing opponent instead of a target, a significant majority of the soldiers revert to a posturing mode in which they fire over their enemy's heads. What was required was conditioning, in the Pavlovian sense, for soldiers to load and fire completely automatically and without thinking, even under the stress of combat. This conditioning is accomplished through thousands of hours of repetitive drilling paired with intense stress and the ever-present incentive of penalty for failure to perform correctly.

Does self-assuredness come from the knowledge of one's demonstrated abilities to manage danger and fear? Is the shared ability to face danger and risk at the root of bonding in military and paramilitary groups? When it comes to killing, Grossman suggests that there is a psychological force at play, one that is stronger than drill routines, stronger than peer pressure, even stronger than the self-preservation instinct. The biggest factor that increases killing is clear, direct orders to do so coupled with strong respect and identification with the leader. Soldiers must bond to their leader just as they must bond to their group. The leader's influence can be enormous. Leaders with legitimate, societally sanctioned authority have great influence over their soldiers, and legitimate, lawful demands are more likely to be obeyed than illegal or unanticipated demands. This integration of the individual into the group is so strong sometimes that the group's destruction—by force or captivity—may lead to depression and subsequent suicide according to Grossman.

Groups also enable killing by developing in their members a sense of anonymity. Psychologists have long understood that a diffusion of responsibility can be caused by the anonymity created in a crowd.[lxv] It has been demonstrated in literally dozens of studies that bystanders are less likely to interfere in a situation in direct relationship to the numbers who are witnessing the circumstance. Thus, in large crowds, horrendous crimes can occur, but the likelihood of a bystander interfering is very low. However, if the bystander is alone and is faced with a circumstance in which there is no one else to diffuse the responsibility to, then the probability of intervention is very high. It is this same process that enables military units to engage in acts that they would never dream of doing as individuals.

The influence of groups on killing occurs through a strange and powerful interaction of accountability and anonymity. Among groups in combat, this accountability to one's buddies and anonymity to reduce one's sense of personal responsibility for kill-ing combines to play a significant role in enabling killing. This may also explain continued loyalty to military units and buddies long after they leave. It is the only place where they can find legiti-macy for the things they did in uniform.

We know from studies of various groups that the more mem-bers, the more psychologically bonded they are to the group, and the closer proximity of the leader, the more powerful the enabling for violence can be. Still, the individual must identify with and be bonded with a group that has a legitimate demand for violence. This power of anonymity in military and paramilitary groups can readily be seen on Canadian streets during protests or group clashes where police often arrive equipped with combat gear rem-iniscent of soldiers, absent of identifying marks or name tags. It raises a significant risk of behaviors that can occur because of the protection of impunity.

Another key element for interpersonal violence is emotion-al distance—dehumanizing others makes it easier to kill them. Cultural distance, such as racial and ethnic differences, also per-mits combatants to dehumanize their victims; the same is true for moral distance, which takes into consideration moral superiority and demonizing identified enemies; for social distance, the im-pact of a lifetime of practice in thinking of a particular class as less than human; and for mechanical distance, which includes the in-fluence of sterile computer-based training, thermal sights, sniper sights, or some other mechanical buffer that denies the humanity of intended targets.

Soldiers trained this way often report after killing in combat that they just carried out the correct drills and completed it be-fore they realized that they were not in a simulator or on a range; however, the deaths of friends and comrades can paralyze and emotionally defeat soldiers. There are circumstances reported to me where soldiers have reacted in anger—a well-recognized reaction to death—making subsequent killing much easier. This does not make them psychopathic killers. But it represents a capacity for the level-headed participation in combat that the rest of us glorify and that cinematic characterizations would have us believe that all soldiers possess. Most soldiers possess another capacity: the presence of empathy for other people—aggression and the presence of empathy can result in inner turmoil after the fact, whereas aggression and the absence of empathy is described as sociopathy. Most of the people we see are decidedly among the former group. Grossman also described another warrior type, not recognized in the psychological community—the metaphoric sheepdogs—because this personality type does not represent pathology or disorder. Indeed, they are valuable and contributing members of our society, and it is only in times of strive that these characteristics can be observed. These people are always vigilant, but they would never misuse their aggression any more than a sheepdog would turn on his flock. In their hearts, however, many of them yearn for a righteous battle, a wolf upon whom to legitimately and lawfully turn their skills.

As I stated earlier, the military and now other first-response organizations have embraced the notion of self-stigma to explain ongoing mental struggles of soldiers and other first responders. But, in my mind, this so-called self-stigma is also a by-product of conditioning via the adoption of the military ethos, traditional value systems, and the promise of specialness that reinforces a narcissistic preoccupation. The line between confidence and assuredness is easily crossed, leading to self-absorption and the belief that one is privileged and above the rules and social mores of common people.

The seeds of narcissism in military people and other first responders may be present before they enroll; this could be in reaction to damaged self-worth and further developed as a defensive response against constant fears of failure—I am special, I can do this, I cannot freeze or fuck up. Our assessments of thousands of military personnel over the years show mild to moderate elevations in these personality traits, including narcissistic ones. But this does not mean that we simply define them as narcissists either. There is a distinction to be made between fundamental narcissism and what is often referred to as a fragile subtype. Among the fragile or brittle narcissists, assuredness and even cockiness are often projected publicly, but privately they understand this to be a public performance. Often, fragile narcissists don't really believe some of the things that they say about themselves. We must remember that their worth is contingent on the whims of their groups and their leaders. The overwhelming majority of them are not typical or full-blown narcissistic personalities—those people perpetually and acutely occupied with their reputations and self-worth and who demonstrate wanton disregard for other people. Our public institutions cannot afford to have many of them around.

Conversely, narcissistic traits appear to be a defensive reaction—part of their personal shields—to help them manage performance anxieties. To meet extraordinary demands, it seems essential for them to hold onto and demonstrate exaggerated beliefs about their abilities as superwarriors. As clinicians, we end up with the responsibility and often the privilege of helping them rediscover the real people behind their military personas—often sensitive and considerate men and women who simply wanted to be acknowledged for doing difficult jobs to the best of their abilities. The real work is to help them integrate these qualities with some of their military qualities toward a balanced understanding of what it means to be a strong and capable man or woman.

On the surface, military personnel who come forward with OSIs often appear to lack fundamental humility because it is equated with weakness and lack of worth as a person. In many cases, I believe this to be a compensatory projection. It is quite possible that other soldiers who were not traumatized represent those who were content to do the best job possible and were not tempted by the demand for perfection—the B-level soldiers. In sum, those people most affected by their military service may have joined to solve a different problem—to prove their basic value as a person from earlier questions about their worth. Many of them come from various family structures that can expose them to fundamental questions about self-worth. Many of them were also severely affected by these early experiences and made adaptations. They toughened up to survive in a lonely world—and in that process, they honed skills that are suited to military life. Regardless of their early lives or their military experiences, however, when they can risk trusting enough to tolerate genuine connection with others without reacting with too much shame or self-recrimination, they can benefit greatly from support and connection with other people.

Those people who were raised by self-centered parents—not necessarily abusive—seem to also seek out specialness to live up to expectations placed on them. This is quite relevant for those people who grew up in military families. They can appear to be incredibly rigid and self-centered and have little tolerance for things like humility, self-compassion, or self-reflection. Through military training, codes, values, and ideals, everyone ends up cocreating personality structures that are a bit of an aberration. It can look like a type of extended adolescent, narcissistic egoism. I realize that this characterization may sound pejorative, but I believe it relates to the phenomenon of one's personal value being based primarily on the reactions and opinions of others.

Prepared alertness seems to be constant for most military people—everything is done with a sense of purpose. Military people gain worth through their actions, and many people over the course of their careers serve multiple and overlapping roles because of our problems with undermanning. They are used to being needed—essential personnel—but when they leave the military, they lose this sense of purpose. While military husbands and wives are certainly missed, family adaptations mean that they are not essential to functioning of the system. Role reorganization within families often means that veterans are perceived by spouses and grown children as barging in and attempting to take over without being asked. It is often a source of significant conflict and adds to their loss of purpose. They feel that they are not needed...just like a bump on a log.

When military members and veterans realize the loss of specialness, their pride can come back to attack them in unforgiving waves: "I was part of a QRF [quick reaction force] in Afghanistan...I was the guy who protected the troops on the ground...I was always looking out for my guys...I saw and did things that most people cannot even imagine...I was JTF [joint task force] and can't ever tell anybody what we did." Receiving a mental-health diagnosis can be taken as an insult—a slap in the face to earned specialness. Successful efforts to help veterans may help them to mentally recondition—to rewire their brains—toward a different personality structure.

This may seem insensitive, but a diagnosis of military PTSD often serves an unacknowledged function for some people. In a peculiar twist, it can become another manifestation of a continued need to be special. These are strong words, but my experience working with veterans struggling with fundamental issues around self-worth points to this dynamic. They steadfastly hold onto a

PTSD label despite the progress they make in resolving critical events. Their reluctance in accepting recovery seems to be driven by a fear that without the label of mentally wounded veteran they may have nothing at all. Sometimes family members realize this and resent these veterans because all efforts leave them feeling helpless. This veteran may habitually grunt when asked to participate in family responsibilities, preferring to spend his days in his "cave" reminiscing or may decide to disappear for days without communicating with anybody. When challenged, he or she will move immediately to argumentativeness or silence. This behavior reminds me of clients who grew up in abusive environments. Sure, they have all reason to be wary of people, to be hypersensitive about trust, and to fear abandonment. But, efforts by well-meaning people to care, give advice, or challenge disagreeable behaviors are often met with extreme reactions. Predictably, other people walk away and leave them, blow up when they have reached their limits, or lie to placate them. So, their behaviors and interactions keep recreating their worlds of repeated abandonment and mistrust of other people. The analogy is the same for military veterans; their sullenness, vacillating moods, and lack of involvement often compound their very issues around self-worth and purpose.

JTF, CSOR, SAR, Royals, Patricias, Dragoons, or *Van Doos*—these are all common Canadian acronyms denoting elite units and storied regiments. Each of them has its own ways of making members feel more important than everyone else. Special berets and uniform tabs—everyone knows that you are special. Ribbons and medals, all proudly displayed for everyone to see. A military identification card, special security classifications, access to secret places where others cannot go. Members are often acknowledged and maybe even thanked by strangers. It is easy to become arrogant, especially when it can help one survive in difficult situations. As

I have suggested, the difference between healthy and toxic narcissism appears to come down to the ability to have empathy for other people—to view and perceive the world through another person's eyes. Those who can stay buoyed by their inflated sense of superiority will appear fine, but when things spiral out of control, depression will often be the reason for seeking help.

In a prospective study by Bachar and colleagues, narcissistic vulnerability was found to predict PTSD over 80 percent of the time.[lxvi] These individuals are believed to be prone to PTSD after an exposure to a traumatic event because they experience the event as a blow to their illusion of invulnerability. They often hate dependence on others and hide their incessant need to be special. They have an exaggerated self-image based on an underlying conviction of relative omnipotence. Traumatic events can undermine their self-image as strong, brave, courageous, and capable of standing up to and resisting any stress or danger. After the traumatic event, they can face feelings of inadequacy or fear. Their sense of uniqueness and invulnerability can be shattered, and they are often forced to feel as ordinary and vulnerable as other people.

Most of us have mild traits of narcissism; a certain degree of self-interest is healthy and demonstrates good psychological health. We all start out life as narcissistic infants, completely self-absorbed and ruled by impulses. Infants, obviously, are incapable of anything more. As we gain a sense of ourselves in relation to others, we are required to outgrow this level of self-absorption. The narcissistically preoccupied person tends to view the world and events happening to him or her through a self-centered lens. They are prone to overreacting to criticism and respond poorly during stressful times. They can fall into feelings of hopelessness or rage in response to failures or rejection and often feel invincible when they meet with victory.

Fifteen

Hero to Zero

"I don't care what his problems are; I want him gone from my ship and gone from the navy." The executive officer could barely contain his contempt for this sailor and quickly overruled efforts to help him salvage his career. The "Jimmy" (naval slang for executive officer) was adamant that his senior communicator was now persona non grata. We had spent a lot of time with Dan, a petty officer, first class and senior communicator on his ship. He had run into problems with gambling and now cocaine use following his deployment to the Gulf; he was struggling with memories of the dead bodies—young, old, male, female, entire families—rotting in the sun.

He was now in a free fall from grace; his senior leadership took it personally. He had betrayed their trust, and in their eyes, he could never be forgiven. They were taking all kinds of actions to ignore and circumvent our efforts to protect his mental well-being. Even a recommendation for a shore posting was overturned. They seemed intent to hurt him personally in return. He had been exemplary in his performance; his prior occupation as a jumper with the airborne meant that he had high standards. And, because of his role, he shared many secrets with the commanding officer and had gained his personal confidence and was even a confidante at times during the deployment to the Gulf.

Dan had been promoted quickly because of his enthusiasm and his commitment to his new trade. He was a quick study. He had been able to forget his previous life as a young paratrooper in East Africa in the early 1990s. But the Persian Gulf had brought some of that stuff back—the smells of death and decay as they patrolled up and down the coastline. He worked nonstop to keep it all together.

In the psychiatric literature, there is the notion of the fragile narcissist. These people are hypothesized to experience alternating feelings of grandiosity and inadequacy. They tend to be unhappy, critical of others, anxious, envious, competitive, and have extreme reactions to perceived slights or criticism. Fragile narcissism is characterized by grandiosity that serves a defensive function, warding off painful feelings of inadequacy, anxiety, and loneliness. The fragile narcissist wants to feel important and privileged, and when defenses are operating effectively, he does. However, when the defenses fail, there is a powerful undercurrent of negative affect and feelings of inadequacy, often accompanied by rage. To be clear, there is nothing wrong with wanting to stand out. This drive serves as the basis of meaning and prepares youth for the demands of adulthood responsibilities. Military and paramilitary environments can prolong and amplify this period through its attention to physical prowess and aggression. The problem for those who abruptly lose this specialness is that the vacuum can leave them with the sense that life has no purpose at all.

Sixteen

If It Bleeds, It Leads

Metallica hammers melodically in the background; Peter sits staring at the wall, lost to time and place. He is in Afghanistan watching an old man writhing in pain by the side of a road through his camera lens. The scene he is capturing is peripheral to his main job of documenting Canadian soldiers tasked with reconstruction efforts. The old fellow had been caught in crossfire between a suspected Taliban sniper and Canadian soldiers; the ongoing threat left no choice but to leave him to bleed out. Peter's brain was telling him to swing his viewfinder around, but he was compelled to keep focusing on this doomed stranger. He couldn't understand why. After all, this footage would never get by public affairs, and it would certainly never see the light of day back home in Canada. Jeez, was he just going to add this one to his private house of horrors? His mental movie theater was already overflowing.

Peter was a seasoned reporter. He had honed his skills and reputation as a major crime reporter over decades back in Canada. First on the scene of gruesome accidents, multiple murder scenes, gang killings, fire fatalities, children dredged up from the bottom of rivers and lakes—he was the guy who got the call to pack his stuff and head out for the lead stories. He was proud of the reputation—the guy everyone called when they needed to capture gut-wrenching reactions from devastated and shocked parents and family members of the dead and injured. The more emotion he could get from people, the better to feed the news-cycle machine. Peter was relentless in capturing people at their most vulnerable moments. He had to be an actor, sharing their grief and shock— anything for the story. It got to a point where nothing was off limits because it could always be edited out before going to air.

There was only one problem. Despite the plaques covering his walls for exceptional reporting over the years, he despised himself! He was nothing more than a chaser of human suffering driven by a killer instinct. Was it in the interests of journalistic truth? He was not sure anymore because it all just seemed to feed into darkness—a raging monster that he could awaken with the help of Metallica. It scared him. Death, mayhem, suicide, blood, and despair could all erupt in a disorganized mess in his head. He often needed his pills to calm down afterward. But he was never going to let anybody tell him that he had lost his edge for the job. He would just control the monster and feed the machine through his developed informants, police contacts, and his own scanner that always alerted him to the next tragedy. More! More! More! Hetfield is still belting as Peter comes out of this morning's trance: "Life, it seems, will fade away…Drifting further every day…Getting lost within myself…Nothing matters…"

In terms of Peter's mental health, he had been diagnosed with severe PTSD and severe depression. Despite medications and talk therapy, he continued to experience debilitating dissociative episodes that could last up to several hours. During these "trances" he would lose touch with his surroundings and the passage of time until he emerged on the other side, sometimes sweating and shaking and at other times numb and physically exhausted. In the formal mental-health world, the newest iteration of *DSM* pays particular attention to this issue of dissociation. There is a vague understanding that these experiences signal pathological biological processes even though these have yet to be identified. However, another way to view dissociative reactions is to understand them as learned behaviors, often initiated in childhood, to self-manage overwhelming emotional reactions. It can even be understood to be a type of "psychic freezing" in efforts to maintain mental stability in reaction to intense psychological pain.[lxvii] In Peter's case, it seemed that checking out mentally helped him manage intense self-recriminations for his role as a journalist reporting numerous terrible events. They helped avoid the incessant urges to end his life.

When we think about the effects of tragedy on the lives of first responders, we typically focus on wars and those who fight them, and rightly so. Sometimes, we pay attention to the innocents who are in the wrong place at the wrong time, but we seldom talk about those people who act as our witnesses—those people who report them. Journalists and reporters who are also in physical and psychological harm's way at home and abroad are somehow invisible because they are not the story: "I thought the camera lens would protect me from all that carnage and death, but man I was wrong. Every image, every devastated mother or father are all stored in my head."

People in search of specialness will go to extremes to fulfill this basic need—never let anybody down, never admit to vulnerability, and never admit to needing anything from others. On the surface, they may appear as incredibly resilient and hardy, but they are often secretly preoccupied with constant anxiety—the fear of falling from grace leads to a driven obsession with perfectionism, self-reliance, and independence—all the prized qualities among first responders of all types. As a military sergeant said to me years ago, "Man, give me an OCD [obsessive-compulsive disorder] type anytime; you can always count on them to get shit done." These are essential qualities for most first-response organizations because of how they are constructed and managed. The downside for many, however, is that the personal mission for specialness fails to deliver, ultimately—there will come a time when every go-to person will run out of steam to be replaced by a bright, new special person. It must be this way. Either exceptional demands wear them out or their protective veneers come crashing down, as if they have fallen into an abyss without the skills necessary to get back out. Climbing back out means trying desperately to get back their former standing, unfortunately. Especially, since the requirement to rely on others and admit to personal limitations is unpalatable.

Standing out from the pack and being treated as special by superiors and colleagues in the military and other places fulfills a primary goal—since you can be counted on, the expectation is that you will always say yes to the next thing asked of you, no matter the request. That's just how people operate, whether it is a friend or a superior. If you are trusted and dependable, you can automatically become the go-to guy/gal. And, make no mistake, this is a wonderful position to be placed in—it is like having perpetual access to a drug that brightens your very existence, generalizing to other areas of life. It can be like living forever on the top of a mountain. Few are brave enough to risk the loss of specialness and a seeming demotion down to the level of everyone else. I believe that this is particularly true for people with fundamental questions about self-worth. Specialness seems to work by soothing narcissistic wounds leftover from things like abuse, neglect, childhood poverty, or bullying. Among the people I know, it seems that most of these special ones do come from stressful backgrounds and join the military to repair leftover wounds to their self-worth. The cruel irony of course is that this can set them up for much deeper wounding.

Life presents us with a series of problems to solve. And, we can look at personality structures as habitual efforts to solve these problems. We become the perfectionist to meet expectations and approval from parents, we learn to shut down and keep emotional upset to ourselves to fit in with family dynamics, or we act out to gain attention since anything is better than invisibility. We need to be seen as a person, to be cherished, to be the most important person to someone, anyone. And, when people see no reasonable or acceptable avenue to receive recognition, they find other ways to solve the problem—it can be teenage pregnancy, gang involvement, joining a counterculture, or entering organizations that provide the promise of specialness—health professions, law, first responders—each replete with people attempting to solve the problem of invisibility and not being seen in the world.

From what I have seen, the ones with the biggest preoccupation with self-worth are the ones most likely to chase specialness at any personal or relationship cost. They are often exceptional, highly competent people who seem driven by their roles. They are essential within their units, even when they are not the designated leader—they improve morale, they serve as a rallying point, and they automatically take control when needed. Everything they have seems to be invested in their reputations. The ones who seem to take the biggest falls (e.g., have chronic PTSD) are the ones who face the loss of reputation. Any behavior on their part that was less than perfect or that ended with the spotlight shifting to the newest rising star can be devastating. After all, leaders are always on the lookout for new people because of operational needs. It can often lay open a psychological injury among the vulnerable that cannot be acknowledged.

This focus on specialness is not exclusive to the military. We must also consider the role of parents and of a society that reveres heroes and promotes specialness. Whether it is within the military, police, medicine, or firefighters, the promise of being needed and being special is seductive and difficult to resist. We hold these roles in a very high level of regard. Nothing wrong with this arrangement because it allows for the maintenance of our complex society. I am suggesting that there can be an incredible downside when these identified special people face very human needs. They often have no audience for the personal costs of these roles even if they were willing to admit to them.

In some respects, special roles are counterfeit avenues to adulthood—an empty promise. Why is it that military personnel continue to experience mental declines independent of deployments, that suicide among health-care clinicians is high, and that interpersonal abuses in first-response organizations cannot seem to be tackled effectively? We must first recognize that the military and other organizations are not completely divorced from civil society. These institutions are also microcosms and arenas where societal contradictions are continually played out—ambivalence over the uses and containment of aggression, our preoccupation with secrecy around the maltreatment of others, our indifference over the place of minorities in power structures or the place of women as valued leaders, the experience of white males seemingly losing their place within traditional social power structures, our deep religious and cultural differences across the country, and our continued preoccupation with relevance in the world. Hero worship helps to keep these other things out of our awareness.

Regrettably, many of our fallen heroes end up doing the unimaginable by ending their lives. Suicide remains a taboo topic in many corners. It is left to people designated as unique "specialists" to speak with authority about what to do. There are elaborate programs designed to prevent people from taking their own lives—a bit hubristic and overzealous. The fact is that humans have taken their lives for all kinds of reasons for millennia—for altruistic reasons, to avoid public shaming, or to end pain and suffering. Most of the people we have seen over the years reported various degrees of suicidality, especially if they felt trapped or faced powerlessness to change things.

Seventeen

Welcome to the Machine

Those who have followed the career of Pink Floyd may remember Roger Waters's famous lament: "Welcome, my son...welcome to the machine." *Indoctrination into the military*, on the surface of it, is a benign term. But recruits are faced with one major task—to relinquish their individuality and their identity as a civilian. This process is completed using various strategies, including being cut off from the outside world, facing continual scrutiny, and being subject to language that holds the threat of public shaming. Many of our current training NCOs served deployments in Afghanistan and are chosen as the best among their peers to guide the next generation of military leaders. They are direct, demanding, and informed by the intensity of war when dealing with recruit mistakes or oversights. Everything is meant to toughen recruits, to awaken them to their own aggressive potential, and to remake them into self-reliant and obedient members. The point of folding one's clothing in perfect squares, meticulously cleaning a living cubicle, standing at attention for long periods of time, or learning to march in a coordinated fashion are intended for mental training and not these specific skills, per se. Training exercises are meant for other purposes—introducing members to incessant pressure to determine mental breaking points and to teach them to subjugate their minds and their physical bodies to external commands. While this process certainly results in self-discipline, this is also a by-product of the primary intent—to condition members to automatically relinquish control to those in command in the service of group needs. "Our jobs are to remake you into something useful in a very short time…" There are few reprieves in this environment, there are no sanctuaries from scrutiny by instructors and fellow recruits, especially when individual failures can result in group punishment and the withholding of earned rewards. As a former Princes Patricia's Canadian Light Infantry soldier told me, "We are only as strong as the weakest link… Nobody wants to be the *zunter, chuggernut, numpty,* or *shit-pump.*"

For those people who have no experience with interpersonal mistreatment, insults, or shaming, the experience can be foreign and overwhelming. I have seen men now in their thirties, forties, and older who grapple with the things that happened to them during their basic recruit training. Of course, it is extremely difficult to attribute their current life circumstances to things that happened decades previously. But the reality for some is that it set their lives on different trajectories. This is especially true for those who were tagged as duds, dykes, or fags. Some of them have sought compensation and legal recourse even decades after leaving the military. If these "failed youth" happened to come from strong military families or communities, it is predictable that they were quietly shunned upon their return home.

For all its success in making reliable combatants, our failure to acknowledge the downside of military training needs to come to an end as we pay attention to the topic of military mental health. I wonder whether we hold a responsibility to help these people reconcile the gaps between who they were before joining, the things they gave up or the loss of themselves, or how they go about retrieving aspects of the person they were before joining. As I have said elsewhere, many of our current understandings and approaches to military mental health end up trying to solve the wrong problem.

Fear of public shaming is the number one concern for most of us. It is one of the oldest forms of social control that ensures compliance with group expectations. For anyone wearing a military uniform or any uniform, the risk of embarrassment or even humiliation is heightened because punishment is swift and often carried out in front of others. From the early days of basic training onward, we adapt by developing a personal shield to reduce the risks of being emotionally or psychologically harmed—we separate from our internal worlds. Some people develop such a toughened exterior that they become entirely different people from the one known by parents or spouses. The soldier may recognize this metamorphosis, but she also develops a range of rationalizations for why she has changed. Many do not recognize these changes because they are gradual and insidious. No matter how harsh the comment, they develop immunity by essentially shutting down and cutting themselves off from everyone.

In the 2013 Canadian Forces Mental Health Survey, the rate of PTSD nearly doubled between 2002 and 2013, with 16.5 percent of CF members surveyed reporting depression, PTSD, generalized anxiety disorder, panic disorder, or alcohol use or dependence. This survey also found that nearly half of regular force members (48.4 percent) met criteria for one of five mental or alcohol-related disorders at some point in their lives. As we know, many of these Afghanistan veterans have faced medical release without any real opportunity to prepare for civilian life.

When it comes to reentering society following war, Sebastian Junger discussed ancient and aboriginal rituals that served to cleanse returning warriors before they were permitted to reenter their communities. Likewise, in her review of previous warrior cultures, Karen O'Donnell recounted how various societies developed specific rituals to aid warriors when they returned from war.[lxviii] For example, in Rome, returning soldiers were bathed to purge them of the corruption of war, Maasai warriors of East Africa underwent purification rites, and Native Americans held sweat lodges to purify warriors from their "inner pollution." Among the Hebrews, soldiers were required to purify themselves before entering back into camps after battle. These practices also found their way into Christian penances. In medieval warfare, all those who fought in battle were required to confess their sins, receive absolution, and make an outward expression of their repentance, even those soldiers who did not kill. Those who did kill were required to undertake extra penances.

These requirements seem obviously connected to the need to assuage a sense of guilt and culpability—giving relief from shame. These ancient cultures may have understood something fundamental about returning soldiers and trauma. They mobilized cultural rituals to help heal traumatic ruptures. These responses seem anchored to the prototypal notion of citizen soldiers who returned to their former communities. Given the segregated and secretive world of today's soldiers, the practicality of these types of responses is debatable. Even so, the idea of helping soldiers to decompress and reorient themselves following deployments and service might be worth consideration.

In a recent study of nearly sixty-seven-hundred full-time Canadian military personnel, 18 percent of soldiers who were deployed to Afghanistan in 2012 had diagnosable mental-health problems.[lxix] Child abuse accounted for 59 percent of posttraumatic stress disorders, 51 percent of panic disorders, and 37 percent of major depression. In fact, those who deployed were nearly two and a half times more likely to have experienced child abuse compared to nondeployed personnel. This latter finding may be of crucial importance. In keeping with my main point, it raises a question about whether ACE people seek out the ultimate test of war for personal reasons—in the interests of self-worth and specialness.

Eighteen
When Life Loses Meaning

The moon's rays slice through horizontal slits in the window blind, forming intricate patterns dancing on the floor. A clock ticks its way through the night, oblivious to the figure positioned on the sofa. Bob's death would be announced later that day by Betty's hysterical screaming. She had just returned home from a week with her sister already anxious because Bob had not answered any of yesterday's phone calls. The official notice of death would state that Bob had died because of a seizure.

Bob had been my client on and off for about five years prior to his death. He had struggled to come to terms with what had happened to him in Bosnia and in his last year had started to grapple with memories of sexual abuse by his older brother. As a master warrant officer in Bosnia, he had been humiliated in front of the troops. His major had ordered him to take control of a convoy move down into a valley and was bombarded with shellfire while the officer moved to the rear: "I had absolutely no idea of what to do or even the orders to give. I was a goddamned Supply Tech, not a grunt. No matter how long I am out, I can't get past the embarrassment…That guy destroyed me." The sad irony is that Bob was afraid to stop drinking because of fears that he might kill himself. So, every day meant a quart of rum for maintenance, and on some days he drank more. He had decided to surprise his wife by being sober when she got back home and probably to also comply with the many suggestions I had made to him over the years about the effects of drinking on his physical health.

⌣⟶

We don't like it when people talk about taking their own lives. We want to intervene, and as care providers and even as friends and family we have a responsibility to convince those with suicidal thoughts about the value of life and about the temporariness of their current level of distress. We can't understand why they do not value their own lives. Apart from our professional obligations, I think we also want to value life so as not to diminish the value of our own lives. Unfortunately, some soldiers and military veterans conclude that their lives are futile, and they are not convinced by our interventions or by our well-intentioned concern for them. We conduct forensic death reviews in efforts to learn from their deaths and to answer liability questions. I don't know if Bob would have been able to come to terms with the awful things done to him in his life. And I don't know if he would have gone on to take his own life when he did not have the buffering effects of alcohol.

It is early winter of 2017 as I begin writing this book. My province and the veteran community have been faced with the tragic deaths of an Afghanistan veteran and his entire family. Once again PTSD and military veterans captured media attention for a brief time before fading once again from public discussion. In the past couple of weeks, suicide reports of young recruits at St. Jean, PQ, and several veterans, including one who had written about his struggles with VAC, have hit the newspapers. Again, there was a refocus on bureaucratic gaps and available treatment programs; unfortunately, and predictably, more involved discussion about the true nature of military trauma was lost within the overarching PTSD cliché.

Moral injury is thought to be a subjective reaction in contrast to PTSD, which is believed to be biologically rooted. In my experience and according to findings in recent literature, this distinction seems arbitrary and misleading, since it is based on a contested hypothesis that PTSD originates within specific brain structures.[lxx] In fact, nearly all cases of PTSD we have treated contain a moral dilemma for the sufferer. "Moral injury is the damage done to one's conscience or moral compass when that person perpetrates, witnesses, or fails to prevent acts that transgress their own moral and ethical values or codes of conduct. Within the context of military service, particularly regarding the experience of war, 'moral injury' refers to the emotional and spiritual impact of participating in, witnessing, and/or being victimized by actions and behaviors that violate a service member's core moral values and behavioral expectations of self or others. Moral injury almost always pivots with the dimension of time: moral codes evolve alongside identities, and transitions inform perspectives that form new conclusions about old events."[lxxi]

Lieberman's recent book *Social*[lxxii] raises troubling questions about the effects of moral dilemmas for military and other first responders. Indeed, the requirements to live in perpetual self-control and self-restraint to deal with society's emergencies and underbelly may be contributing to the problems of addiction and suicide within these groups. The alternative would be to live according to their own impulses, urges, and desires, which might better serve them but not necessarily serve their immediate groups or society's interests. There is an inherent trade-off required to participate in first-responder roles. They must put their own interests and sometimes their own integrity aside to accomplish the things expected of them. Self-control makes society happy but not the individual members.

A relevant question is whether operational-stress injuries amount to the cumulative price of self-restraint in terms of interfering with experiences of emotional connection and meaning. In cases where we are effective in helping with military PTSD, I believe it is because helpers can temporarily breach these adopted emotional straightjackets to uncover suppressed or warded off desires and impulses without raising their fear of losing control, being judged, or shamed. In fact, even though they are described as negative strategies, based on the work of Davidson and Begley,[lxxiii] things like alcohol, drugs, or gambling may be so attractive because they serve to temporarily take our mental braking system offline, allowing soldiers and others relief from their emotional pressure cookers. Even so, these types of experiences are usually not enough. Conversely, to benefit from emotional decompression, veterans may need the experience of relinquishing overcontrol and emotional restraint and to test it out repeatedly in different interpersonal settings to overcome military conditioning effects. I do believe that this is essentially about rewiring their neural networks in a process similar to learning to drive or play an instrument.

According to Davidson and Begley, one of the emotional styles is sensitivity to context, which involves the hippocampus—a brain structure involved in memory and personal contextual information. In military PTSD veterans, reduced hippocampal volume has been found repeatedly and had been found to be predictive of

PTSD. This reduction in volume has been related to a "tuned out" emotional style used to explain loss of context among military veterans. An important question is whether specific conditioning tactics and expectations of military personnel in emotional avoidance and suppression can contribute to this tuned-out emotional style. This may be particularly relevant to military populations when we consider that the average recruit is between the ages of eighteen and twenty-four. Given our knowledge that the PFC (prefrontal cortex) does not fully develop until approximately twenty-five years of age, I think we should consider whether military enrollment for young recruits constitutes an important aspect of their development rivaling the influences of their preservice families.

As reported by Davidson and Begley, weakened connections between emotional centers and the PFC are linked to insensitivity to context. So repeated experiences of emotional suppression may contribute to a weakening of neurobiological pathways between the hippocampus and the PFC, in essence taking the braking system off inputs from the amygdala and the limbic system: "The circuitry of the emotional brain often overlaps with that of the rational, thinking brain—and I think there is a strong message in that: Emotion works with cognition in an integrated and seamless way to enable us to navigate the world of relationships, work, and spiritual growth" (p. 89).

In sum, a feeling state permeates almost everything we do and virtually all areas of the brain are involved, not just one structure or another. When it comes to genetic determinism to explain mental-health problems, Davidson and Begley provide reviews of numerous studies attempting to argue for genetic explanations for things like male aggression, criminality, depression, and introversion. In all cases, they found that whether prospective genes were turned on or off was determined by early developmental experiences—especially the experience of childhood abuse: "Child abuse alters the expression of genes in the brain, this altered expression impairs the ability to cope with adversity, and the inability to cope with adversity leaves the individual more vulnerable to suicide" (p. 101).

In terms of context, our politicians and bureaucrats have been forced to respond to military suicides amid a plethora of theories attempting to explain the plight of these men and women. Theories about preexisting conditions (e.g., childhood abuse or neglect), concurrent stressors (family pressures and financial distress), disordered brains, and even self-stigma (self-critique and denial of problems) have all been advanced as possible causes. But we do not consider the effects of the military work and conditioning environments. They are somehow off-limits as a consideration. We do not appear to be willing to explore the actual day-to-day context of first-response workplaces, including the operating value systems, the consequences of basic conditioning models, unspoken but shared codes of "manly" conduct, and supervisory practices as possible sources of distress.

In the increasingly demanding workplaces of first responders and the military, there is considerable attention to professionalism. It is important to be highly skilled, but I think we risk turning these environments into soulless and rationalized places where the only thing that matters is one's ability to do the job. There is not much leniency or time to treat coworkers as human beings. In fact, workplace relatedness is increasingly mediated through formal human resource policies and procedures. There is not much room for people to have a bad day or to be emotionally upset following a bad call because of organizational pressures and paranoia over public scrutiny and possible legal actions. Workplaces can turn into emotional pressure cookers—a working wasteland.

We might benefit from a little less focus on "what's his problem" and a little more attention to "what's our problem." This could go a long way in reminding everyone that at the end of the day we are all just human—nothing more, nothing less. If we were to approach a distressed colleague and focus on the things that are being done or not done within the group instead of focusing on the individual's weakness, we might end up with a very different understanding of first-responder mental health.

Within neuropsychology, Donald Hebb's seminal work has had lasting effects on our understanding of the processes involved in learning.[lxxiv] A now famous phrase has been attributed to his theories: namely, *neurons that fire together wire together.* Put simply, repeated learning trials result in the development of vast arrays of interconnected neural networks. The kinds of things we learn, our actions, and the ways in which we think, then, can reorganize the brain itself—we create anxious brains and we create aggressive ones as well. When it comes to serious mental-health problems, the great news from neuroplasticity and epigenetic research is that just as learning wires the brain in specific patterns, new learning can also reverse or rewire the brain to other states by creating new pathways or resurrecting dormant ones. This is the point of education and military conditioning, even though it may not be considered in these terms—repeated learning trials under specific conditions can rewire the brain. In terms of effective mental-health interventions, the same processes are likely occurring, only in reverse.

These lessons are at the heart of trauma interventions. For example, the practice of teaching people how to experience deep relaxation before they begin discussing distressing issues is meant to pair absence of fear with memories of distressing events. There are a number of forces at play, but the central underlying principle can be explained by Hebb's theories of learning. Other strategies like opposite action (e.g., Marsha Linehan's work in Dialectical Behavior Therapy) direct anxious people to resist the temptation to withdraw and instead to make efforts to engage other people. Those people who are practiced worriers seem to benefit from things like mindfulness and meditation to retrain the vigilant brain. Similarly, those people who habitually avoid emotion seem to benefit from the simple act of privately naming their emotional experiences. It is essential for veterans and others to not be seduced by misguided messages from well-meaning but incorrect clinicians who tell their clients to learn to live with symptoms because they will not change—everything we know about learning indicates that this is simply not true.

Military conditioning amounts to the acquisition of an automated mental skill set, and when seen through the lens of neuroplasticity, it suggests that their brains are reshaped and rewired. In fact, based on the works of researchers like Ledoux and Lieberman, it appears that repeated experiences of emotional suppression may weaken connections between the PFC and other emotional brain centers. While soldiers are required to focus exclusively on rationality, they may be simultaneously weakening neural pathways to their emotional centers. Hence, those people who interpret anxiety and strong emotional reactions as signs of impending doom or cardiac problems may have lost the ability to interpret internal physical sensations as signals of their emotional health. Instead, they focus on rational thought processes without the benefit of emotional inputs. If we accept that the physical body is the basic reference point for emotional awareness, we must consider the effects of teaching people to ignore, control, deny, and push past their physical reactions. The emerging research seems to lead us to an important conclusion—namely, that new, altered pathways develop during intense military conditioning.

In terms of recovery from trauma, however, for rewiring to occur, learning trials in emotional and physical awareness and self-regulation need to be repeated and reinforced so that they are eventually automated. In other words, in somewhat mechanistic language, new reactions need to become hardwired to replace those overlearned in the military. In short, the goal of maintaining good emotional health for military people and first responders presents significant challenges to deeply embedded institutional values around meaning systems—being a reliable soldier or being an effective leader. Current foci on resilience and mental health will likely necessitate a serious reconsideration of the very fabric of these institutions for the potential of real and sustained change.

In reviewing the influence of neurobiological reactions, in his recent book *Anxious,* Joseph LeDoux clarifies a misinterpretation of his prior work—namely, a structural misnomer that amygdala dysfunction is at the root of PTSD. He argues convincingly that this brain structure is simply a component of a larger threat detection system whose main role is to continually monitor the environment. When the system perceives changes and possible threats that can be out of conscious awareness, impulses are forwarded to the biological system for preparation state, and, relatively speaking, later these signals inform the cognitive system for evaluation. And as I understand his argument, here is the key: The way in which we cognitively interpret physiological signals is based on our prior learning and contextual information in determining how we respond. If I am running and feel my heart pounding rapidly, I accept and interpret this physiological reaction as normal. If I am walking down a street at night and experience the same physiological reaction in the absence of immediate explanation, I would very likely begin scanning the environment for a possible threat source automatically. If none is found, many people will continue scanning and likely shift toward internal focus on the operation of their biological system. This person may notice stomach upset from an earlier meal or may flash to a memory of being mugged on a dark street decades ago. The type A, pragmatic, focused person may have a much harder time unraveling the impact of emotional cues on their physiological reactions, which is also the basis of panic disorder—biological reactivity without explanation, where fear can build upon fear.

Lieberman goes so far as to argue that our brains are designed intrinsically as a social organ. Specific regions, notably the dorsal anterior cingulate cortex and insula of the brain, in fact, interpret social pain (i.e., disapproval and rejection) in the same way as physical pain. He outlined a line of inquiry based on functional magnetic resonance imaging studies to support his main argument. Lieberman makes a vital observation—the self-restraint required for socialization to one's group has profound impact on neurological functioning. The opposite, of course, is to give into one's hedonistic impulses. These observations are extremely informative when it comes to understanding mental unwellness among all first responders. Namely, as populations under constant self-restraint, we must wonder about the cumulative effects on their emotional processing capabilities.

Some veterans decide to maintain self-restraint and do not risk emotional decompression because of a basic fear of losing control. Other veterans have told me that on the heels of Afghanistan, cocaine use has been on a steady rise among soldiers. Given cocaine's physiological stimulant effects, this should not be surprising. Among the well-established effects of this drug are increases in one's sense of self-esteem and power, providing a way to recreate the heightened sense of self and specialness they experienced on deployments.

I think an important question centers on acceptable outlets for military veterans to loosen high levels of self-restraint without fears of losing complete control. On the surface, one might think that mental-health settings might be the answer, but they are often tightly scripted and emotionally regimented settings. The reality is that many distressed soldiers continue to seek relief from self-restraint by using various substances while they are under medical care. Some of the lucky ones may find helpers who are comfortable with emotional exploration/expression and who engage them directly instead of strictly adhering to rational, scripted interventions.

Leaving the military means having to learn a new structure, one that accommodates spontaneity, uncertainty, anonymity, taking risks, and the requirement to assert oneself in the world. Excessive self-restraint can be a formidable obstacle. The latter point of assertiveness is an ongoing challenge for many veterans and indeed for most people. Often, they jump quickly between passivity (shutdown) and aggression (hyperalertness). Instead, assertiveness hinges on the ability to acknowledge one's vulnerability while also establishing one's needs and personal boundaries with other people—interacting with others in genuine and honest ways.

So, it seems to me that a key component of understanding mental distress is understanding and accounting for the role of emotions. In *The Emotional Life of Your Brain*[lxxv], Davidson and Begley make the point that contrary to ideas promoted within psychology, the prefrontal cortex is not devoted exclusively to reason. It is also the seat of both positive and negative emotions. And, as advanced by Lieberman, the supposed site of emotion, the limbic system, is simply another component of the threat-detection system, and, furthermore, physical and emotional pain systems in the brain are highly interrelated. This partially explains the main source of pain in our present-day lives—social pain (e.g., rejection).

Traumatic stressors have faced us as a species since our beginnings—death from predators of all types, starvation, or natural calamities—which forced us to band together for survival. We learned to interact and to huddle in small groups enabling us to thrive as a species. We became social beings out of necessity. We know from numerous studies that the issue of PTSD is not reducible to the frequency or intensity of traumatic exposures; instead, the PTSD problem seems to come down to nonrecovery among some people who can't seem to benefit from the security of their primary groups.

When veterans leave their sections, platoons, and units—their community of comrades in arms—they can face additional disconnection and invisibility, and I believe that this is the real challenge facing veterans. We are now beginning to describe this as transitional strain. To understand this phenomenon, we should acknowledge—as described by James Wright—that military veterans are increasingly separated from and unrepresentative of the larger civilian population. These factors increase the likelihood of invisibility both during service and afterward. This reality is often lost in clichéd conversations about PTSD. Somehow, we forget that veterans come from our communities; they are our sons and daughters, our parents or our neighbors. They remain steeped in values of stoicism and self-discipline: silent and invisible citizens.

Nineteen

Help Me Find the Way Back Home

*I didn't find out only about PTSD; I
found out how to be human again.*

—ARMY VETERAN

Culture shock is a subcategory of a more universal construct often termed *transition shock*. It can be described as a state of loss and disorientation predicated by a change in one's familiar environment that requires adjustment. A related issue, normlessness derives partly from conditions of complexity and conflict in which individuals become unclear about social norms. Sudden and abrupt changes occur in life and the norms that usually operate may no longer seem adequate as guidelines for conduct. In this context, then, the so-called mental diseases may represent manifestations of culturally appropriate ways of signaling mental-emotional distress.

When I think about it, the things common to distressed Canadians include behaviors like social withdrawal, emotional shutdown, cycling between irritability and apology, obsessing over personal failures, and projecting into the future. These ways of experiencing upset are usually highly coordinated with social expectations, social mores, and hence may be considered a social signaling behavior. Together, they seem to reflect a problem of social isolation. Missing from our accepted notions of mental distress are fundamental questions about the social reinforcements for these behaviors, how they serve the person and his group, and the benefits and downsides of these signaling behaviors to others. My experience has taught me that at the heart of every trauma, including military ones, is an irreconcilable conflict—a values conflict between what did happen (i.e., sanctioned military action) and what should have happened (i.e., personal conscience). Lost in the gap between these extremes are the things that often drive external signs of distress. For example, many veterans describe engaging in things while soaked in an adrenaline high and then reviewing these things obsessively when they come back out of the situation and begin to calm down. It is only when people have reached some level of stability and safety that what actually happened begins to sink home.

It is sometimes said by critics of the military that we are simply brainwashed. If this is the case, then, I think we must include the impact of our national narrative on military mental health. We are all brainwashed to some extent by Canadian pride and nationalism; our children may be particularly vulnerable to this. In fact, we know that many people who join the military come from military families and the cadet movement; our national stories are steeped in history of our war heroes. However, I do believe that ACE recruits may be more susceptible to the effects of military training partly because of damaged self-worth and partly because they already use things like emotional suppression, compartmentalization, and various dissociative strategies to manage strong emotional reactions. Of course, there are also many ACE people who are as tough as nails and excel in their military roles. These self-contained curmudgeon types are often needed by their groups as safety valves and morale boosters. They can be the court jesters willing to say and do the things that the rest of the group is unwilling to say or do. After all, every now and then, every institution needs someone to remind the emperor that he is naked!

In 2015, I conducted a study of ACE-OSI veterans and found that, compared to other veterans with PTSD, this group was more likely to suppress emotional reactions, had a higher incidence of substance abuse, and displayed higher use of dissociative strategies to manage themselves.[lxxvi] Later, many of them also agreed to participate in a developmentally focused PTSD group therapy program. Most of them did exceptionally well; many no longer met PTSD status at the end of the program. They could do one thing in particular—openly explore and share with others the impact of all major life events. Veterans may be well served by coming together in groups instead of working individually, which calls into question our preference for individual-focused interventions.

We are not at a point of having open and frank discussions about ACE veterans within the memberships of our front-line institutions. Be that as it may, our current predicament over military and veterans suicide suggests that we need to revisit the accepted war trauma narrative. We certainly must avoid secretly blaming these men and women as spoiled goods coming into the military. A glaring fact in Canada is that over one-third of all children experience abuse and neglect; in the United States, this is estimated to be closer to one-half of all children. They are overrepresented within our military, with recent estimates at 50 percent of serving members.

When it comes to the issue of brainwashing—often described by psychologists as thought reform and social influence—there are questions about its reliability and effectiveness. Social influence happens all the time throughout our lives; it underpins the notions of socialization in families, schools, playgrounds, peer groups, and workplaces. It represents the collection of formal and informal ways in which those in authority change other people's attitudes, beliefs, and behaviors. It can also be broken further into its constituent forces: compliance, persuasion, and education. Brainwashing can be understood as social influence by combining these components with the threat of punishment coupled with isolation and dependency on those in charge. These environments exert complete control over the person—sleep patterns, eating, access to bathrooms, and meeting other basic human needs. The aim is to break down the subject's basic identity and then replace it with desired behaviors, attitudes, and beliefs for the current environment. When it comes to military and paramilitary conditioning, there is little doubt about the use of many of these strategies, but it does not seem that brainwashing effects are permanent. Many experts believe that even under ideal conditions, the effects are often short term—the person's old identity is never fully eradicated but instead is hidden away so that the person appears to be a true believer. So, once the adopted identity stops serving the person or they are no longer reinforced with reward or threats of punishment, they often revert to former self. Again, the effectiveness of these strategies seems to come down to personal vulnerabilities to influence. One of the real consequences for susceptible military personal is the threat of self-betrayal: "Agree with us that you are lazy/undisciplined/not worthy and that you need to be taught these things." Family, friends, and peers are seen to be holding a wrong belief system—they are less than us. This rejection of one's beliefs and former family values can produce crisis and internal conflicts as members attempt to adjust to military life. Carl Castro reported a spike in adjustment problems and suicides during the first several years of military service in the United States. "Who am I, where am I, and what am I supposed to do?" These questions speak to a crisis of identity that can lead to mental-health problems like social anxiety, depression, and substance abuse. Ironically, in gregarious settings, new members can experience profound loneliness. Sadly, it is often the same process in reverse when veterans attempt to reenter civilian culture at the ends of their careers. But this time there are no structured, all-encompassing processes to reverse these former processes. When it comes to those people who experienced complicated attachment patterns, it is predictable that they will likely experience significant dislocation when they leave the structure of the military since they have no acceptable prior identity base. Their real mission for joining fails them.

There are recent clear signals of a developing maturity within our military institution. It is no longer the place I served where we were expected and even encouraged to work hard and play harder. There are many who would point out that the institution has resisted change. There is certainly truth to this observation. But the continued maturation of the institution will be reflected in the diversity and health of its membership.

Epilogue

It is paradoxical that many of the young men and women who were the least protected as children often end up in social protector roles. Many of them seem fully prepared mentally and emotionally for occupations that demand toughness and self-reliance because of their earlier life experiences. About half of our military membership grew up in these stressed environments. We do not have estimates on the number of personnel who grew up in immediate or extended military families or the overlap between abuse histories and military lineage. It would be a mistake to think that they all end up as mental-health casualties. Nor can we presume that they all experience chronic mental struggles—many soldiers and veterans seem to benefit greatly from relatively brief interventions and move on with their lives. Furthermore, I believe we would be heading in the wrong direction by mistakenly viewing mental declines in the military and other first-response roles as deficits in things like hardiness or resilience. On the contrary, if there is a deficit it seems to amount to an inability to develop genuine trust with other people.

It does seem that we are on the verge of a new era when it comes to understanding the mental health of first responders. There has been a recent acknowledgment of complex relationships between challenged childhoods and the incidence of mental-health problems among these people; however, we must continually resist the temptation of treating these members as aberrant or damaged due to preexisting injuries. After all, they are represented in all ranks throughout the military and other first-response organizations. Many of the people we have seen were superb soldiers and leaders, and it is not until they experience challenges to their self-worth—the loss of specialness—that they begin to decline, sometimes dramatically.

My intention has not been to criticize the military or other first-response organizations or even the ways in which they condition and prepare young men and women to take on the responsibilities for extraordinary roles. My concern is directed to the potential repercussions of this conditioning when these people are worn down or they leave their employment and attempt to adjust to routine civilian life. We expend considerable resources indoctrinating and mentoring people into their roles, but to date we have paid little attention to the process of leaving. We know that the two-year postrelease time frame is an especially disorienting and risky time for many veterans, including those who are not medically released. We may need to rethink the processes of how and when people officially leave the military. It might even require that they remain as nondeployable paid members to allow them time and training opportunities to truly decompress and prepare mentally for civilian life.

In retrospect, when our military developed the *Joint Personnel Support Unit* concept some years ago I must say that I was quite excited about the possibilities; a colleague and I even volunteered to provide assistance locally with no success. I continue to believe that it could have provided an ideal opportunity for soldiers to engage in mental reconditioning to bring their careers to a close. There could have been extended and focused opportunities to help them psychologically prepare for civilian life by reevaluating the usefulness of codes and ideals they had taken on over the years. They could have been provided opportunities to appreciate the impact of their entire careers—both good and bad—and to begin making decisions about the type of man or woman they wanted to be in retirement. It could have also provided opportunities for well-organized exit interviews to help them bring closure to their careers. Unfortunately, it appears that this initiative will end before any of these things can be realized. I think it was a concept ahead of its time that ended ultimately as a missed opportunity.

As it stands, in terms of formal system responses, there is much focus on occupational health to enable people to continue to serve, there are specific interventions to assist people who may have been harmed by specific duties, and there are a wide range of administrative and legal avenues to report abuses and grievances. We have not discussed the range of potential negative effects of military conditioning and possible remediation necessary to mentally prepare veterans to reenter civil society.

Nearly all our information and research on military mental-health and operational-stress problems has been informed by the American experience. We attempt to extrapolate its relevance to the Canadian situation. In many cases, it is helpful, and at other times it simply does not reflect the Canadian context. There are major ideological differences between the US military and our own, even though there are many examples of shared training and joint operations. Among these differences is the sheer size of the US military compared with our relatively small military and their many experiences in active war zones. The US military is described by many as the best-trained military force globally. The caricature of the US military is one that is driven ideologically by deference to God and country and unfaltering patriotism. Their role as the de facto global police force seems to take on an almost crusade-like quality in advancing the highest of American values. Canadian soldiers, on the other hand, have been described as tenacious and adaptable fighters, always punching above their weight and often irreverent when it comes to ideologies. In some cases, we have been described as brash and undisciplined, which ironically is an incredible source of pride among our soldiers who perceive them-selves as versatile and adaptable. They interpret these qualities as the ability to think and respond to situations on the ground, even if this means countermanding orders given from the rear. Canadian soldiers take on qualities of bravado, pride, and loyalty, and some of these qualities have implications for the transition to civilian life. We need to come to a better understanding of their real mental-health struggles. As one veteran of Bosnia and Afghanistan said to me during a recent research study: "Going through the process of having mental problems, getting diagnosed, treated, and released medically because of PTSD is soul destroying. Any questions about my life now and my future are irrelevant."

Like our approach to addiction in the military years ago, mental-health treatment compliance and success status have been confounded with workplace performance. This hyperconcern over institutional liability, which is a legitimate issue, has also pre-maturely ended the careers of many soldiers. The resulting ero-sion and destruction of their military identity—their shields—can leave veterans helpless and hopeless in the larger world. These un-spoken reactions to medical diagnoses speak to an aspect of transi-tion that can easily be missed by administrators and clinicians.

As it stands, we have no proven ways within formal mental health to help military members reconstitute their core sense of identity. After all, we are often unwittingly complicit in unraveling it in the first place. It can be a profound loss followed by an anomic life unless we begin putting in place those things aimed at repairing identity, creating an alternate identity that does not hinge solely on pride. This might require us to have conversations about the inadequacies of formal mental health in addressing military values and a cultivated sense of specialness. It may require us to help veterans understand the personal costs they paid in the name of service to country.

Once veterans realize that their most basic military values are incompatible with civilian life, many of them predictably and inevitably question almost everything they did in uniform. This can happen after a specific operational event, at the end of a mission, and especially when they leave the institution. They are alone and many of them feel duped as exemplified by the following: "They broke me and then threw me on the scrap heap." This sentiment is extremely difficult for serving members to hear or for the leadership and politicians to acknowledge because it points to fundamental gaps in how we understand their struggles. These reactions are also difficult for clinicians to understand. On the heels of the Afghanistan War, many Canadian veterans continue to voice these sentiments, leaving those with vested interest in maintaining the existing framework to ignore, control, or marginalize their voices. These people shake the very foundation of military service, which relies on the invocation of overused clichés and mantras.

For my part, if we were to truly listen to these people we could get closer to understanding transitional maladjustment among our military and other first-response veterans. As military veterans tell me repeatedly, the Canadian public has been led to believe that the military has an exemplary mental-health system—which is true when compared to civilian systems—but average people don't appreciate the arbitrariness of this support. Access to care can depend on the personal opinions, biases, and the budget considerations of various base surgeons across the country or the expectation that contracted clinicians scrutinize the motives of personnel who come forward for help often resulting in contests between patients and clinicians. As an army veteran said to me, "To get help you have to tell them that you are desperate and can't function, but when you do that you can basically say good-bye to your job. If you tell them that you have problems, but they are not extreme, then you get no help. It's a catch-twenty-two, and the everyday Joe doesn't get this."

How is it that caring helpers can be so seemingly callous? Maybe because of our unrealistic professional training and the disconnect with the reality of military patients, maybe because of pressures from employers to quickly return people to operational roles or to recommend their removal, maybe because our accepted interventions are not suited to many military personnel, or maybe because of inherent power differentials where civilian clinicians take on hierarchical characteristics of their military employer without even realizing it. A colleague several years ago relayed the following to me, after meeting with a young medical officer: "I am improving the mental health of the military, one release at a time."

If we are intent on discharging mentally damaged veterans into the civilian world, we need to be honest about the benefits and the downsides of our socially segregated military and conditioned warrior mentality. The truth is that we are all vulnerable, specialness is temporary, we all need other people, adrenaline mode is for the young, nobody is "ten feet tall," and emotional connection to others is the basis of purpose and personal meaning. The real message to be learned from traumatic stress reactions including PTSD may be that anything that separates us psychologically from our iden- tified groups can result in mental deterioration. Whether this is through self-judgment, outrage, fears of public shaming, guilt, or loss of the belief in special abilities compared to other members of the group, the real injury seems to be separation/isolation— first mentally/emotionally and then predictably through physical separation. In a real sense, physical separation by choice is reflec- tive of psychological separation. Fundamental mistrust of others may have been there all along but not really tested in a world of pseudorelationships until self-reliance fails them. The risk of our standard ways of helping is that they can exacerbate a tendency toward self-centeredness—a preoccupation with dysfunction and potential threats and reduced engagement.

It is easy to recast military and veterans as an idealized ver- sion of World War II vets rather than engage them as real people with real-life problems, many of which are shared by the rest of us. With a smaller and smaller military, this population continues to become more homogenous—many of them come from families with a historical connection to the military. We risk ending up with transgenerational military lineage. This is not necessarily bad, but it is not representative of the accepted notion of citizen soldiers either. This situation can be described as a somewhat incestuous, self-maintaining culture. For many members, the military as it ex- ists, with its particular values and expectations, is all they have ever known.

People who have experienced chronic abuse or neglect learn one fundamental lesson—that they are essentially alone in the world. They learn to survive alone, and the evidence of overactive neurophysiology may simply reflect this reality. These vigilant and hyperactive brains can serve them exceptionally well in military and other first-responder roles. Even so, investigations of adult PTSD (e.g., functional magnetic resonance brain scans) continue to try to link structural brain changes with recent events; the possibility of neurological changes reflective of adaptations to military conditioning have not been explored. So, brain hyperactivity may very well reflect their normal functioning and may have very little to offer in explaining current distress reactions. Indeed, as argued by Lieberman, when we are not occupied with things in our external environments, our brain reverts to its default network—preoccupation with our social sphere. For example, we think about our relationships and our reputations, we replay aspects of interactions, or we envision how we might handle an upcoming meeting with someone.

When soldiers and veterans come out of adrenaline mode—either by choice or by sheer exhaustion—to be faced with the pace and rhythm of normal life, they must contend with themselves. Many of them fear this above all else, and it may be too much to ask them to do this entirely on their own. Whether they like it or not, they face questions over the meaning of their military service and indeed with the meaning of their lives. The place of specialness, entitlement as identified heroes, and aggression as central underpinnings of relationships also have to be addressed if they are to move forward in their lives. As I see it, within the context of a larger world they have to decide just like the rest of us what it means for them to be a good man or woman. This shift toward a balanced civilian identity requires us to acknowledge vulnerabilities—including emotional ones—and taking the risk to be honest about the things we carry that separates us from other people.

And, the real answer to my daughter's question—I was too preoccupied with anger over wounded pride to remember the importance of humility.

Endnotes

i.   S. Bulmer and D. Jackson, "You Do not Live in My Skin: Embodiment, Voice and the Veteran," *Critical Military Studies* 2, no. 1–2 (2016): 25–40, https://doi.org/10.1080/23337486.2015.1118799.

ii. M. Maya Eichler and J. L. Wiebe, "The Art of Discomfort: Engaging in Dialogue on War," *Critical Military Studies*, forthcoming.

iii. T. O. Afifi, Taillieu, T., Zamorski, M. A., Sarah Turner, Kristene Cheung, Jitender Sareen, "Association of Child Abuse Exposure with Suicidal Ideation, Suicide Plans, and Suicide Attempts in Military Personnel and the General Population in Canada," *JAMA Psychiatry* 73, no. 3 (2016): 229–38.

iv. G. Goldstein, *War and Gender: How Gender Shapes the War System and Vice Versa* (Cambridge: Cambridge University Press, 2001).

v.   H. Jung, "Can the Canadian Forces Reflect Canadian Society?," *Canadian Military Journal* 8, no. 3 (2007): 27–36.

vi. H. M. Moss, *Manliness and Militarism: Educating Young Boys in Ontario for War* (Toronto: Oxford University Press, 2001).

vii. http://www.militaryheritage.com/nwmp.htm, accessed August 30, 2017.

viii.   http://blogs.britannica.com/2009/02/beyond-darwin-eugenics-social-darwinism-and-the-social-theory-of-the-natural-selection-of-humans, accessed August 30, 2017.

ix.   M. Eichler, *Militarizing Men: Gender, Conscription, and War in Post-Soviet Russia* (Stanford, CA: Stanford University Press, 2012).

x.   L. Cooper, N. Caddick, L. Godier, A. Cooper, and M. Fossey, "Transition from the Military into Civilian Life: An Exploration of Cultural Competence," *Armed Forces & Society* 2016 (2016): 1–22, https://doi.org/10.1177/0095327X16675965.

xi.   M. Jakupcak, T. L. Osborne, S. Michael, J. Cook, and M. McFall, "Implications of Masculine Gender Role Stress in Male Veterans with Posttraumatic Stress Disorder," *Psychology of Men & Masculinity* 7, no. 4 (2006): 203–11.

xii.   J. Fox and B. Pease, "Military Deployment, Masculinity and Trauma: Reviewing the Connections," *Journal of Men's Studies* 20, no. 1 (2012): 16–31.

xiii.   S. Withworth, *Men, Militarism, and UN Peacekeeping: A Gendered Analysis* (London: Lynne Reinner Publications, 2004).

xiv.   C. Ciaran Kovach, "How Important Are Masculinity and Femininity in the Culture of Militaries?," *Journal of International Affairs* 2015/2016, no. 1 (2016): 1–2.

xv.   L. Gouliquer, "Soldiering in the Canadian Forces: How and Why Gender Counts!" (Unpublished Master's Thesis, Department of Sociology, McGill University, Montreal, 2011).

xvi.   G. Hofstede, *Masculinity and Femininity: The Taboo Dimension of National Cultures* (London: Sage Publications, 1998).

xvii. R. G. Maunder, J. Halpern, B. Schwartz, and M. Gurevich, "Symptoms and Responses to Critical Incidents in Paramedics Who Have Experienced Childhood Abuse and Neglect," *Emergency Medical Journal* 29 (2012): 222–7.

xviii. V. M. Follette, M. M. Polusny, and K. Milbeck, "Mental Health and Law Enforcement Professionals: Trauma History, Psychological Symptoms, and Impact of Providing Services to Child Sexual Abuse Survivors," *Professional Psychology: Research and Practice* 25, no. 3 (1994): 275–82.

xix.   L. M. Candib, J. Savageau, A. L. Weinreb, and G. Reed, "Inquiring into Our Past: When the Doctor Is a Survivor of Abuse," *Family Medicine* 44, no. 6 (2012): 416–24.

xx.   J. J. Whelan, "Exploring the Relationships between Untreated Adverse Childhood Events and Substance Abuse, and their Impact on PTSD Relapse Rates among Canadian Military Veterans," in *Beyond the Line: Military and Veteran Health Research*, eds. A. B. Aiken and A. H. Belanger, 180–95 (Kingston, ON: McGill-Queens University Press, 2013).

xxi.   J. J. Whelan, "Effects of Developmental Abuse and Symptom Suppression among Traumatized Veterans," *Psychology* 6 (2015): 540–48, https://doi.org/10.4236/psych.2015.65052.

xxii.   M. D. Lieberman, *Social: Why Our Brains Are Wired to Connect* (New York: Crown Publishers, 2013).

xxiii.   J. Cacioppo, "How to Break the Dangerous Cycle of Loneliness," Citylab, accessed August 30, 2017, www.citylab.com/navigator/2017/04/how-to-break-the-dangerous-cycle-of-loneliness/522180/.

xxiv.   A. Lucksted and A. L. Drapalski, "Self-Stigma Regarding Mental Illness: Definition, Impact, and Relationship to Societal Stigma," *Psychiatric Rehabilitation Journal* 38, no. 2 (2015): 99.

xxv.   C. B. Fjeldheim, J. Nöthling, K. Pretorius, M. Basson, K. Ganasen, R. Heneke, K. J. Cloete, and S. Seedat, "Trauma Exposure, Posttraumatic Stress Disorder and the Effect of Explanatory Variables in Paramedic Trainees," *BMC Emergency Medicine* 14 (2014): 11.

xxvi.   J. Shay, "Moral Injury," *Psychoanalytic Psychology* 31, no. 2 (2014): 182–91.

xxvii.   E. Becker, *The Denial of Death* (New York: Macmillan Publishing, 1973).

xxviii. Ibid.

xxix. C. W. Hoge, *Once a Warrior Always a Warrior: Navigating the Transition from Combat to Home Including Combat Stress, PTSD, and mTBI* (Guilford, CT: Globe Pequot Press Life, 2010).

xxx. E. Bachar, H. Hadar, and A. Y. Shalev, "Narcissistic Vulnerability and the Development of PTSD: A Prospective Study," *Journal of Nervous and Mental Disorders* 193 (2005): 762–65.

xxxi. M. Cousineau, *Further Than Yesterday: That's All That Counts* (Self-published, 2015).

xxxii. C. R. Figley, *Treating Compassion Fatigue* (New York: Routledge, 2013).

xxxiii. E. Erikson and J. Erikson, "On Generativity and Identity: From a Conversation with Erik and Joan Erikson," *Harvard Educational Review* 51, no. 2 (1981): 249–69.

xxxiv. E. Erikson, *Identity, Youth, and Crisis* (New York: Norton, 1968).

xxxv. D. Grossman, *On Killing: The Psychological Costs of Learning to Kill in War and Society* (New York: Back Bay Books, 2009).

xxxvi. J. LeDoux, *Anxious: Using the Brain to Understand and Treat Fear and Anxiety* (New York: Viking, 2015).

xxxvii. Lieberman, *Social*.

xxxviii. S. W. Porges, *The Polyvagal Theory: Neurophysiological Foundations of Emotions, Attachment, Communication, Self-Regulation* (New York: Norton, 2011).

xxxix. R. J. Davidson and S. Begley, *The Emotional Life of Your Brain: How Its Unique Patterns Affect the Way You Think, Feel, and Live and How You Can Change* (New York: Penguin, 2012).

xl. J. J. Whelan, *Ghost in the Ranks: Forgotten Voices and Military Mental Health* (Vancouver, BC: FriesenPress, 2016).

xli. Government of Canada, *Mental Health of Canadian Veterans: A Family Purpose.* Report of the Standing Committee on Veterans Affairs. Ottawa, ON, June 2017.

xlii. Australian Institute of Health and Welfare, *Incidence of Suicide among Serving and Ex-Serving Australian Defence Force Personnel 2001–2014.* Cat. no. PHE 213 (Canberra: AIHW, 2017).

xliii. L. Van Til, J. Sweet, A. Poirier, K. McKinnon, K. Sudom, S. Dursun, and D. Pedlar, *Well-Being of Canadian Regular Force Veterans, Findings from the LASS 2016 Survey* (Charlottetown, PE: Research Directorate, Veterans Affairs Canada. Research Directorate Technical Report, 2017).

xliv. J. Thompson, M. B. MacLean, , L. Van Til, K. Sudom, J. Sweet, A. Poirier, J. Adams, V. Horton C. Campbell, and D. Pedlar, *Survey on Transition to Civilian Life: Report on Regular Force Veterans* (Ottawa: Research Directorate,

Veterans Affairs Canada, and Director General Military Personnel Research and Analysis, Department of National Defence, 2011).

xlv.   Van Til et al., *Well-Being of Canadian Regular Force Veterans, Findings.*

xlvi.   S. Junger, *Tribe: On Homecoming and Belonging* (New York: Hatchette Book Group, 2016).

xlvii.   H. Pope, G. R. Olivardia, and K. A. Phillips, *The Adonis Complex: How to Identify, Treat and Prevent Body Obsession in Men and Boys* (New York: Touchstone, 2002).

xlviii. https://www.brookings.edu/blog/brookings-now/2017/03/23/working-class-white-americans-are-now-dying-in-middle-age-at-faster-rates-than-minority-groups, accessed August 30, 2017.

xlix.   D. Bilsker and J. White, "The Silent Epidemic of Male Suicide," *BCMJ* 53, no. 10 (2011): 529–34.

l.   https://earlycanadianhistory.ca/2016/02/01/violence-in-early-canada/, accessed August 30, 2017.

li.   S. R. Razack, *Dark Threats & White Knights: The Somalia Affair, Peacekeeping, and the New Imperialism* (Toronto: University of Toronto Press, 2004).

lii.   P. Stogran, *Rude Awakening: The Government's Secret War against Canada's Veterans* (Vancouver, BC: FriesenPress, 2015).

liii.   M. Friscolanti, "How a Record-breaking Canadian Sniper Kill Shot Was Almost Forgotten," Macleans, 2006, accessed August 30, 2017, http://www.macleans.ca/news/canada/we-were-abandoned/.

liv.   J. Eggenberger, *Understanding Canadian Army Ethos* (London: Royal United Services Institute of Vancouver Island (RUSI-VI), 2004).

lv.   http://www.forces.gc.ca/en/training-ethics/ethics-terms.page#military-ethos, accessed August 30, 2017.

lvi.   L. Festinger, *A Theory of Cognitive Dissonance* (Stanford, CA: Stanford University Press, 1962).

lvii.   http://espritdecorps.ca/moir/2015/4/22/desertion-and-shell-shock, accessed August 30, 2017.

lviii.   N. Bamford, "Seven Things People Miss about Working When They Retire," *Informed Choice: Independent Financial Planning*, 2016.

lix.   http://www.afterpsychotherapy.com/anxiety-symptoms-and-panic-attacks/, accessed August 30, 2017.

lx.   C. Castro, "Military Suicide Transition Theory, the Hemingway Effect and the…," YouTube, accessed August 30, 2017, https://www.youtube.com/watch?v=hCOsUfVtb8A.

lxi.   J. Wright, *Those Who Borne the Battle: A History of America's Wars and Those Who Have Fought Them* (New York: Perseus Books, 2012).

lxii. Jung, "Can the Canadian Forces Reflect Canadian Society?," 28.

lxiii. Bilsker and White, "The Silent Epidemic of Male Suicide."

lxiv. B. Fallon, J. Ma, K. Allan, M. Pillhofer, N. Trocmé, and A. Jud, "Opportunities for Prevention and Intervention with Young Children: Lessons from the Canadian Incidence Study of Reported Child Abuse and Neglect." *Child and Adolescent Psychiatry and Mental Health* 7, no. 1 (2013): 4, https://doi.org/10.1186/1753-2000-7-4.

lxv. J. M. Darley and B. Latané, "Bystander Intervention in Emergencies: Diffusion of Responsibility," *Journal of Personality and Social Psychology* 8 (1968): 377–83, https://doi.org/10.1037/h0025589.

lxvi. Bachar, Hadar, and Shalev, "Narcissistic Vulnerability and the Development of PTSD."

lxvii. C. Hunt, *Transformative Learning through Creative Writing: Exploring the Self in the Learning Process* (New York: Routledge, 2013).

lxviii. https://www.academia.edu/9996461/Post-War Rituals of Return and Reintegration of Warriors, accessed August 30, 2017.

lxix. D. Boulos and M. A. Zamorski, "Contribution of the Mission in Afghanistan to the Burden of Past-Year Mental Disorders in Canadian Armed Forces Personnel," *Canadian Journal of Psychiatry* 61, Suppl. 1 (2016): 64S–76S.

lxx. LeDoux, *Anxious.*

lxxi. http://moralinjuryproject.syr.edu/about-moral-injury/, accessed August 30, 2017.

lxxii. Lieberman, *Social.*

lxxiii. Davidson and Begley, *The Emotional Life of Your Brain.*

lxxiv. D. O. Hebb, *The Organization of Behavior: A Neuropsychological Theory* (New York: John Wiley & Sons, 1949).

lxxv. Davidson and Begley, *The Emotional Life of Your Brain.*

lxxvi. J. J. Whelan, "Effects of Developmental Abuse and Symptom Suppression among Traumatized Veterans."